NEW DIRECTIONS FOR STUDENT SERVICES

John H. Schuh, *Iowa State University*
EDITOR-IN-CHIEF

Elizabeth J. Whitt, *University of Iowa*
ASSOCIATE EDITOR

The Art and Practical Wisdom of Student Affairs Leadership

Jon C. Dalton
Florida State University

Marguerite McClinton
Florida State University

EDITORS

Number 98, Summer 2002

JOSSEY-BASS
A Wiley Company
www.josseybass.com

THE ART AND PRACTICAL WISDOM OF STUDENT AFFAIRS LEADERSHIP
Jon C. Dalton, Marguerite McClinton (eds.)
New Directions for Student Services, no. 98
John H. Schuh, Editor-in-Chief
Elizabeth J. Whitt, Associate Editor

Microfilm copies of issues and articles are available in 16mm and 35mm, as well as microfiche in 105mm, through University Microfilms Inc., 300 North Zeeb Road, Ann Arbor, Michigan 48106-1346.

ISSN 0164-7970   e-ISSN 1536-0695   ISBN 0-7879-6340-2

NEW DIRECTIONS FOR STUDENT SERVICES is part of The Jossey-Bass Higher and Adult Education Series and is published quarterly by Wiley Subscription Services, Inc., a Wiley company, at Jossey-Bass, 989 Market Street, San Francisco, California 94103-1741. Periodicals postage paid at San Francisco, California, and at additional mailing offices. Postmaster: Send address changes to New Directions for Student Services, Jossey-Bass, 989 Market Street, San Francisco, California 94103-1741.

New Directions for Student Services is indexed in College Student Personnel Abstracts and Contents Pages in Education.

SUBSCRIPTIONS cost $65.00 for individuals and $130.00 for institutions, agencies, and libraries. See ordering information page at end of book.

EDITORIAL CORRESPONDENCE should be sent to the Editor-in-Chief, John H. Schuh, N 243 Lagomarcino Hall, Iowa State University, Ames, Iowa 50011

Cover photograph by Wernher Krutein/PHOTOVAULT © 1990.

Jossey-Bass Web address: www.josseybass.com

Manufactured in the United States of America on acid-free recycled paper containing at least 20 percent is postconsumer waste.

CONTENTS

Editors' Notes   1
Jon C. Dalton and Marguerite McClinton

1. The Art and Practical Wisdom of Student Affairs Leadership   3
Jon C. Dalton
The author argues that practical wisdom is the highest achievement of professional practice and examines how practical wisdom is gained and nurtured in professional life.

2. Relationships: The Critical Ties That Bind Professionals   11
Larry Roper
Cultivating successful relationships is an essential skill of effective leadership. The author examines how successful student affairs leaders nurture and sustain professional relationships.

3. Reflections on Career Development Among Student Affairs Leaders   27
Gregory S. Blimling
Student affairs professionals develop their careers in many intentional and serendipitous ways. Monograph authors reflect on their career journeys and the wisdom they have gained about the success they have achieved.

4. Managing Change in Student Affairs Leadership Roles   37
Jon C. Dalton and Diana Imanuel Gardner
Managing change is one of the most complex skills of leadership. This chapter examines some of the most difficult changes confronted by student affairs leaders and the practical wisdom they have gained from these encounters.

5. Self-Renewal and Personal Development in Professional Life   49
Linda Reisser
Self-renewal and personal development are necessary for sustained leadership effectiveness. This chapter discusses how senior student affairs administrators keep their busy lives in balance.

6. The Moral Domain of Student Affairs Leadership   61
William Thomas
This chapter discusses the pivotal role of values and ethics in professional leadership and how leaders use moral learning and core values to make tough decisions and live a committed life.

7. Uncommon Truths: A Diary of Practical Wisdom 71
Gregory S. Blimling
The author reflects on unconventional truths that he has learned from
over twenty-five years of student affairs administration.

8. Life Planning: Preparing for Transitions and Retirement 83
Elizabeth Nuss and Charles Schroeder
Long-range career planning is difficult in the student affairs profession
because of a lack of clearly defined career tracks and inherent job insecurities. Retirement strategies and other late career options are presented and discussed.

9. Nuggets of Practical Wisdom 95
Jon C. Dalton and Alicia Trexler
This chapter presents a collection of personal maxims and practical
advice contributed by the monograph authors.

10. Concluding Thoughts 101
Jon C. Dalton and Marguerite McClinton
Concluding observations on the role of practical wisdom are provided,
and suggested uses for the content of the monograph are discussed.

INDEX 105

EDITORS' NOTES

In the summer of 2000 I approached a number of student affairs colleagues to ask for their participation in developing a somewhat unusual monograph for the Jossey-Bass New Directions for Student Services series. I asked them each to maintain a journal in which they would record their personal reflections on a number of topics related to practical wisdom in student affairs leadership.

I advised them not to be overly concerned about searching the literature because what I wanted them to do involved a different kind of research effort. Instead, I asked them to make a reflective inward journey to explore the practical wisdom they had learned from their many years of service as student affairs leaders. I explained that I wanted them to try to identify within themselves the best and most abiding personal truths about student affairs leadership. I encouraged them to be as personal and candid in their reflections as they felt comfortable. I knew that asking practitioner-leaders to be so reflective and personal might be quite out of the ordinary, so I did not know what to expect from their introspections.

Over the next six months the reflective pieces began to arrive and I found myself engaged in reading them. They revealed surprising things I did not know about these friends and colleagues. The pieces they wrote were deeply personal and reflective. They wrote about work, values, friendships, and family, about their failures and successes, and about what mattered most to them in their lives and work. They shared stories and experiences and reflected on the personal truths and convictions they had forged from their varied careers in student affairs. Their pieces reflected a shared sense of deep gratitude for a profession that has provided such good and fulfilling work.

It has been a great pleasure to collect and edit these special reflections, stories, and essays on the art and practical wisdom of student affairs leadership. I join my colleagues in offering these personal reflections as gifts to a profession that has enriched our lives and given us so many ways to affect the lives of students in the higher education setting.

Jon C. Dalton
Marguerite McClinton
Editors

JON C. DALTON is associate professor of higher education and director of the Center for the Study of Values in College Student Development at Florida State University.

MARGUERITE MCCLINTON is a first-year higher education doctoral student at Florida State University in the department of educational leadership.

The author argues that practical wisdom is the highest achievement of professional practice and examines how practical wisdom is gained and nurtured in professional life.

The Art and Practical Wisdom of Student Affairs Leadership

Jon C. Dalton

There is an important dimension of leadership not often discussed in the professional literature of student affairs because it is so difficult to define and measure. This dimension or aspect of leadership is practical wisdom. The term *practical wisdom* conjures up images of earlier times, when learning through experience was more revered and leadership was regarded as an achievement one gained through accumulated life experiences and the insights derived from practiced reflection.

The concept of practical wisdom combines two important aspects of competency: (1) sound knowledge and (2) good judgment. Practical wisdom is more than knowledge. It involves the ability to draw upon knowledge selectively and apply it successfully in specific situations (Barnes, 1995). The more narrow domain of intellectual knowledge is often regarded as the most important measure of professional competency, and less attention is given to the domain of good judgment.

Effective long-term success as a student affairs professional requires both sound knowledge and good judgment. We respect and honor those professionals whose expertise and good judgment over time have earned them success in their careers and the respect and admiration of their peers. We will explore in this monograph the practical wisdom of some exceptional student affairs leaders. We will examine their reflections, stories, and personal convictions about what they believe are some of the most important truths of effective professional practice. We will learn from their insights about the relationship between knowledge and good judgment and how an appropriate balance between these two critical dimensions of practical wisdom has enhanced their long-term professional effectiveness and success.

Good judgment is nurtured through experience and refined by insights gained from professional practice and the accumulated convictions about what matters in the routine circumstances of daily work. This type of professional expertise cannot be easily taught because of its highly situational nature. No doubt this is one of the reasons for the heavy focus on objective knowledge and skills in professional education. But the lessons of good judgment can be studied and learned, and we hope this monograph will be useful in this endeavor. Indeed, if we are to be effective in developing student affairs leaders who possess practical wisdom we must better understand how they learn to make good judgments and integrate good judgment with sound professional knowledge.

The practical wisdom and guidance offered here are drawn from the observations of ten student affairs leaders, including the editor, who were asked to compile a series of reflections about their long and successful careers. Their reflections are often personal and anecdotal and are intended to provide for the reader glimpses into the insights and convictions these leaders have gained from professional practice. This monograph will examine in particular the practical wisdom that these student affairs leaders have gained through considerable experience and reflection and how this wisdom has been shaped by their beliefs about some of the most important aspects of student affairs practice today. The practical wisdom they share will be of use to student affairs professionals, graduate students, and others who wish to understand how good judgment and knowledge are integrated in the student affairs profession.

Meanings of *Profession*

There are at least four meanings associated with the word *profession*. The first meaning indicates a type of work or field of activity in which an individual or group of individuals is engaged. Thus, a professional is one who pursues a particular occupation or career for his or her livelihood.

A second meaning of *profession* refers to the beliefs and standards that characterize a field of work. The original meaning of *profession* derived from the vows made by men and women when they entered religious orders. They were expected to state in their vows their commitment to beliefs and practices that would define their new life in the order. Consequently, a *professional* is one who makes a public declaration of beliefs and pledges to work and live by the credo of the profession. Professionals are those who "profess" or vow to practice their expertise in the context of certain defining beliefs and standards of practice.

The third meaning of *profession* refers to special knowledge and training. A professional is one who possesses special expertise gained from advanced study in the field. This expertise may come from special knowledge derived from formal and informal study and also from associated professional clinical and field experiences.

There is also, we would argue, a fourth meaning or connotation of the word *profession*. It refers to the art of making good judgments in the specific decision-making situations of professional practice. We will discuss all four meanings of profession in this monograph, but our emphasis will be upon the second and fourth connotations. We want to examine especially the meaning of practical wisdom from the vantage point of a group of student affairs leaders who have extensive knowledge and skills and have had long tenures of successful professional leadership. We will also explore what these student affairs leaders "profess" as guiding beliefs and standards and how these are integral to the practical wisdom they have gained.

Practical Wisdom Versus Training

Individuals who receive professional training are educated for particular knowledge and competencies in specialized roles. The expertise and competencies of the student affairs profession are defined in a number of ways, including the standards adopted by professional associations such as the National Association of Student Personnel Administrators and the American College Personnel Association, by inter-associational groups such as the Council for the Advancement of Standards, and by graduate professional training programs. The formal standards adopted by these organizations have done much to guide the development and professionalization of work in student services over the past four decades.

Our focus, however, is not primarily on the formal credentials, standards, and training that are used to define the professional knowledge and skills of student affairs fieldwork. These important professional criteria are examined elsewhere in the literature and provide an important foundation of standards and guiding principles for the student affairs profession. The formal standards of education and practice do not, however, fully exhaust the knowledge and skills that turn out to be important for long-term success in the student affairs profession. There are several reasons for this. First, it is ultimately impossible in formal training programs to examine all of the circumstances and tasks that must be managed in a lifetime of changing professional roles and responsibilities. Second, it is extremely difficult for professional educational programs to capture the complex nuances of situations, roles, and relationships that are vital aspects of successful long-term leadership in the student affairs profession. Finally, there is a certain astuteness derived from practicing the craft, a kind of "street smarts" learned from accumulated successes and failures, that is difficult to codify and standardize. This astuteness or practical wisdom is an important aspect of the successful craft of being a student affairs professional. Although it is difficult to objectify, it is possible to learn about the practical wisdom of student affairs leadership through the personal stories, reflections, and insights of those who have practiced the profession successfully over many years.

Practical Wisdom

Practical wisdom is the art of effective student affairs practice. It is the result of three types of learning: (1) academic study, (2) accumulated professional experience, and (3) collaboration and mentoring with colleagues in the profession. Practical wisdom requires the integration of intellectual intelligence and emotional intelligence in order to make effective decisions in the complex circumstances of student affairs work. Student affairs professionals who are successful over a lifetime of leadership are most likely to be those who master essential learning and skills derived from academic study, practical experience, and the shared insights of colleagues in the profession.

Aristotle argued that practical wisdom is achieved only in the interface of reason and emotion (Barnes, 1995). Practical wisdom involves not only an intellectual understanding of what is reasonable to do but also a sense of what is appropriate in particular situations. This sense of what is appropriate to do in particular situations comes primarily from the insights and convictions gained from one's own reflections on practical experiences in addition to the shared wisdom from one's colleagues. This is one of the reasons older professionals, those with more varied and extensive experience, are likely to have more practical wisdom because of their greater appreciation of particular facts and situations (Barnes, 1995).

Inexperienced professionals may have mastered a body of content knowledge and possess technical competency, but they usually have not yet learned how to put such knowledge and techniques into extensive practice because they lack experience with the wide range of particular situations confronted in professional work (Barnes, 1995).

The mark of inexperienced student affairs professionals is an overreliance on intellectual knowledge, on the things one has read or been taught. New professionals tend to diagnose problem situations by relying primarily on objective knowledge. They have not yet learned how to connect this knowledge with the good judgment that comes from dealing with similar situations on many occasions over time. It is one thing, for example, to understand student rights and responsibilities from a technical standpoint when one is involved in a student disciplinary matter; it is something else to recognize what is appropriate to do with regard to a particular student in a particular situation. Having been in such situations many times, even though the particulars vary greatly, gives one a sense of what is appropriate and fitting. Practical wisdom is cultivated slowly through the integration of knowledge and experience and clarified and enriched through interaction with colleagues.

Practical wisdom is a marriage of the habits of the mind and the habits of the heart (Bellah and others, 1985). The habits of the mind include rational thinking skills, the ability to process information, and effective use of technology and information resources. The habits of the mind enable individuals to analyze, interpret, and solve various kinds of problems, but they do not necessarily teach one to be wise, responsible, and prudent. The habits of the heart are a necessary complement to knowledge and intellectual skills; they include moral and emotional qualities that enable one to exercise good judgment in specific situations. Practical wisdom is achieved by integrating cognitive and emotional intelligence. Cognitive skills are filtered and focused through both accumulated experience and emotional sensitivity that is honed by many decisions and situations. Long-term success as a student affairs professional requires habits of both mind and heart. Knowledge and reasoning skills without emotional intelligence probably will not stand the tests of leadership. What is rational is not always what is fitting. "Wisdom is the most finished form of knowledge," wrote Aristotle (Thomson, 1955, p. 211). At the same time, emotional intelligence outside the context of rigorous and disciplined thinking will probably wear thin and become ineffective over time.

Can Practical Wisdom Be Taught?

One of the intriguing questions that we must examine in this volume is whether it is really possible to convey in writing the subtleties and complexities of the practical wisdom of the profession. Is it possible to describe the combination of intellectual and emotional skills and qualities that constitutes practical wisdom? The strict answer must, of course, be no. If practical wisdom were simply a matter of discrete knowledge it could be objectively taught and communicated. It is possible, however, to convey useful insights and perspectives about practical wisdom that can serve as guides or markers for professional development.

The approach we will use in this examination of practical wisdom is to share the stories and personal reflections of successful leaders in the profession about some of the most important aspects of professional practice. Through our personal accounts of challenging situations, reflections on how we grew and learned from leadership successes and failure, and the insights we gained from study, experience, and our colleagues, we hope to provide useful guidance on how to develop practical wisdom in student affairs practice. This approach is similar to mentoring and role modeling in that the emphasis is placed upon learning through interaction and reflection upon the personal experience of others. Mentors and role models teach through the context of their own experience and understanding and invite others to take what is useful and beneficial from their example. Their purpose is not to have any final "answers" but to offer stories, advice, reflections, and their own conduct as personal testimonies to what has worked and not worked for them.

Community of Colleagues

One of the most important resources for learning practical wisdom is the community of professional colleagues. The next best thing to having expertise is the ability to call upon the expertise of friends who work at the same bench. One of the great benefits of participating in professional meetings is the opportunity to interact with and learn from one's colleagues. It is in these interactions that the shared wisdom of the profession is transmitted to newcomers and colleagues. Practical wisdom is difficult to achieve apart from the professional community, since the legacy of wisdom that comes from the experiences and knowledge of so many colleagues is so rich and deep. The wisdom they share comes not only in their formal research and publications but also in their personal stories, conversations, and informal interactions.

When professional communities are organized into formal associations and guilds, they play a valuable role in creating guidelines, standards, and norms to guide professional practice. In this way, the best practices of the profession are collected and communicated as part of an on-going discussion and debate about what it means to be a professional. It is, of course, possible to read about these issues and discussions as a way of staying abreast of professional issues, but there really is no substitute for the personal encounter and interaction that take place when colleagues spend time together, sharing and learning from one another.

The community of colleagues plays another important role. It helps confirm the values and standards that define the moral norms of the professional. Being a professional involves, at least in part, a commitment to a set of ethical standards that guide practice. Professionals who affiliate with professional groups agree, at least tacitly, to be guided in their conduct by the moral norms of the professional group. Consequently, the community of colleagues exerts a moral influence on professionals that is an essential aspect of what it means to be a professional.

For this reason the pursuit of practical wisdom is inescapably a moral enterprise. One cannot gain practical wisdom without an ongoing effort to define and achieve personal moral integrity. The theme of personal integrity is touched on by most of the contributors to this volume because the development of practical wisdom involves so many ethical considerations and character-building situations. Practical wisdom is ultimately impossible without the development of character. The frequent references to moral and ethical issues in the reflections of our contributors indicate that wisdom and ethics are inexorably linked for them as well.

Storytellers

All of the contributors to this volume are leaders in the student affairs profession. They are practitioners and intellectuals who have led student affairs organizations and contributed frequently to the professional literature. All have completed their doctoral degree and most have taught on at least a part-time or adjunct basis. By almost any measure of professional excellence, such as professional publication, campus leadership, awards and reputation, and leadership in professional organizations, these individuals are all outstanding professionals. Moreover, they represent some of the rich diversity of our profession in terms of gender, race, and ethnicity as well as in the types of higher education institutions they serve.

At least from the writers' perspective, the contributors to this monograph represent a sample of the best of our profession. Student affairs staff throughout the profession have greatly benefited from their experience and knowledge. The profession, of course, has many other outstanding colleagues like them; these are but a few. It is our hope that this monograph will encourage attention to the practical wisdom of student affairs leadership and to student affairs leaders who have rich stories and reflections to share about what they have learned over many years in the profession.

References

Barnes, J. *The Cambridge Companion to Aristotle.* Cambridge: Cambridge University Press, 1995.

Bellah, N. B, Madson, R., Sullivan, W. M., Swidler, A., and Tipton, S. M. *Habits of the Heart.* Berkeley: University of California Press, 1985.

Thomson, J. A. *The Ethics of Aristotle.* London: Penguin Books, 1955.

JON C. DALTON is associate professor of higher education and director of the Center for the Study of Values in College Student Development at Florida State University.

2

The author discusses essential principles and skills in developing and managing professional relationships.

Relationships: The Critical Ties That Bind Professionals

Larry Roper

I would argue that our success as student affairs professionals is more closely tied to our ability to construct and manage essential relationships during our careers than to any other activity. Because most of us begin as entry-level professionals there is little question about the need for us to have successful relationships with students. But too often as young professionals we fail to grasp the importance of developing and responsibly managing relationships with faculty colleagues, supervisors, and senior level administrators, among others. We are quick to dismiss the need to develop these key relationships as merely "playing politics" or some other unflattering term. The fact is, many careers are potentially sabotaged because of a lack of sophistication in interpersonal relationships or failure to cultivate connections that can be career sustaining. As good fortune has it, many of us are able to survive and excel in student affairs despite our early awkwardness in relationships. The ineffective social skills that are sometimes tolerated in new and mid-level professionals can be fatal to senior administrators.

The quality of our relationships with others has a powerful impact on our ability to progress and get things done in our institutions. However, because of our focus on task accomplishment we often do not give complete consideration to showing care for relationships. The busyness of our personal and work lives can lead to sloppiness in attending to the needs of others. The challenge before us as student affairs professionals is to develop an approach that places relationships with others at the center of both our personal and professional life. Being thoughtful about the quality of our relationships and showing generosity in our dealings with others are essential components of being effective in life and work. Our personal and professional relationships elicit from us the depth of our capacity to care about others and our ability to be open to their needs. Relationships will challenge the range of our emotions, our ability to persevere with others, and our tolerance for interpersonal chaos.

This chapter will offer the reader a range of perspectives on essential issues in developing and managing professional relationships. The views offered have important themes embedded (implied) within them. These themes and the corollary questions that flow from them can be important guideposts for us as we seek to develop successful relationships: care, communication, trust, commitment to others, generosity, perseverance, integrity, communication. Do we have the ability to create space for others to participate in our life? What personal guiding principles do we have for our relationships? What is relationship integrity? Are we capable of being gracious in the face of tension and conflict? Are we trustworthy? How able are we to struggle with others and on behalf of others?

Developing Relationships

There is no such thing as an unimportant or insignificant relationship. Every person and every interaction matters, though there are clearly differences in the degree to which specific interactions matter. Each human interaction that we have in some way influences how we feel about ourselves, how we are perceived, the success that we achieve, and the legacy that we will leave. Unfortunately, because of the volume of people and issues that we deal with, it is difficult, if not impossible, to fully honor every conversation, communication, and interaction in a way that leaves the other person feeling valued and us feeling successful. Our most successful interactions are generally those in which we are able to achieve full engagement with the other person. The issues that students, other colleagues, and stakeholders bring to us matter significantly to them; therefore it is essential that we develop the skill and ability to be as engaged as possible in those interactions. Full engagement communicates to others that we are focused on them in the conversation and we are interested in them and their issues. As we develop a pattern of consistently successful interactions and demonstrate to those in our communities that we have the capacity to be engaged in the issues that matter to others, we will construct a network of successful relationships and a reputation of caring about others.

A trusted colleague with whom I have worked for the last several years teaches that relationships are not much more than a series of conversations. He believes that the heart of a successful relationship rests in our ability to practice effective communication over time. On one hand, a good relationship is evident by a pattern of consistently successful conversations between the person with whom we are in the relationship and us. On the other hand, a bad relationship is characterized by a history of unsuccessful conversations with and about that other person with whom we are in relationship.

In order to construct a positive relationship it is imperative that we create a history of successful conversations.

Consider this: think of a personal or professional relationship that is important to you but that is not as successful as you would like it to be (a relationship that is not "working" for you). Now think about your last three conversations with or about that person. How would you characterize those conversations?

When most people are confronted with the preceding scenario they express feelings that range from embarrassment to upset. Questions about how we manage conversations with and about those with whom we are struggling to have a successful relationship can be revealing concerning the role that we play in keeping a relationship from moving forward. How we manage conversations about others suggests a great deal about our level of commitment to that other person. In order to be successful in our work we must develop behavior patterns that show our commitment to having successful relationships with students and other colleagues. We should consistently ask ourselves, What do my conversations about those with whom I am in relationship tell others about my commitment to those people? As student affairs professionals, we need a set of tools or concepts that can be accessed to assist us in maintaining positive relationships, improving relationships that are not working, and constructing new relationships.

Every person and organization needs a set of principles that will guide them in interpersonal and organizational relationships. The principles should speak to the values and beliefs from which people will operate in their dealings with others. Principles also provide a mirror against which to reflect in assessing relationship progress. The following is a sampling of relationship principles that have been useful in our organization. The principles are taught as part of a conversation skills workshop that is available to all members of our academic community. The guiding principles include

- Don't start a conversation unless you are committed to the other person
- Listen generously
- Be on each other's side
- Speak your truth
- Take care of the other person
- Stay focused in the conversation and stay in the conversation until it is complete
- Treat the conversation and each person as important
- Be clear about the value that you are producing
- Manage each other's reputation

Don't Start a Conversation Unless You Are Committed to the Other Person. It is important that we not begin a conversation with another person unless we are committed to having the conversation turn out right for them. Too often we enter into conversations and relationships without thinking enough about the other person. If we focus too much on making sure that we come out of the conversations achieving our own goals, we will not be able to leave the other person with a positive experience. We should enter conversations with a commitment that we want the conversation to turn out right for the other person. We would dramatically change the quality of our relationships and conversations if we were to commit that we would not start any conversation unless we are fully committed to the other person. Consider what it means when we engage in conversations with people to whom we are not committed. Our work should be characterized by relationships that reflect care for the other person.

Listen Generously. If we focus more on the quality of our listening we will see a shift in how we relate to others. If we are truly present for another person in a conversation we will listen generously. Generous listening involves applying the most positive intent possible to what the other person shares. We are constantly presented with situations where we have the option of hearing the negative implications in a person's statements or interpreting the comments positively. Through generous listening we commit to those with whom we are in relationship that we listen for their positive intentions and their commitments.

Be on the Other Person's Side. Commitment to others reflects an ability to be on their side. Whether providing negative feedback or congratulating for work well done, we need to let our colleagues know that we are on their side. We have the ability to support others consistently and unconditionally or be situational allies to others. If we want to be seen as being loyal in our relationships we should not adopt behaviors that communicate that we are willing to abandon our colleagues.

Speak Your Truth. Honesty is an essential dimension of successful relationships. The people who are in relationship with us deserve to know how we feel about issues. The challenge is that we should share our personal truth in a way that does not diminish the other person. Each person should cultivate truth-telling as a core dimension of their relationships.

Take Care of the Other Person. When we enter conversations with others we must be fully present to them. Being present means that we are tuned into the needs and feelings of the other person and willing to respond appropriately. Taking care of the other person requires being engaged with where they are emotionally.

Stay Focused in the Conversation Until It Is Complete. If we are to create and sustain successful relationships we must confront the challenge of managing distractions and focus. When we are engaged in conversations it is easy to drift among a variety of topics without bringing closure to any. Successful conversations reflect focus and intention. Successful conversations also reflect perseverance. Regardless of how difficult conversations become, if we are committed to others we will stay engaged in the conversation until we have declared it complete.

Treat the Conversation and Each Person as Important. We will invariably find ourselves in conversations in which we have difficulty connecting with the person or relating to the topic. These are among the most challenging situations we will face in our quest to achieve excellence in our relationships. Being effective in relationships requires that we are able to approach these situations with the same care and interest as those in which we are deeply connected to people and issues.

Be Clear About the Value That You Are Producing. We are not able to be successful at all we attempt. There are times when we will be in conversations or relationships in which we are not capable of producing value. Whether through asking the other person what he or she needs from us or through stating where we think we can be helpful, it is important that we are clear about what values we are bringing into our relationships.

Manage Each Other's Reputation. In every conversation that we have about another person we are either positively managing or mismanaging their reputation. In committed relationships colleagues take responsibility for managing the reputations of others. This requires that we monitor ourselves and interrupt situations in which others try to draw us into conversations that do not treat others well. In the process of managing other's reputations we are also managing our own.

Telling Our Stories

The principles offered above, among others, have been helpful for my colleagues at Oregon State University and me. My colleagues who have contributed to this chapter provide insight into their personal beliefs and approaches to relationships. The following excerpts from their journals vary in form and content, reflecting the diversity of approaches that are accessible to us. The consistent dimension is that each reflects wisdom and humility gained from years of managing challenging professional situations and relationships.

Liz Nuss offers a brief and powerful case situation. The case poses dilemmas and values questions, with the most important question being, Do we ever have the right answer?

> Director X has just called. She has had an unexpected emergency that will require her to be out of the office for several weeks. She is, as might be expected under the circumstances, very upset and emotional. I shift gears from thinking about residence life and begin to ponder how to cover the events and programs in the other unit.
>
> Personnel and supervision issues are the primary challenge in leadership assignments: learning the strengths and limitations of individuals and trying to find the best ways to motivate and challenge them, understanding their learning styles and leadership style, and trying to modify my style to bring out the best in them. Some days I think I have it just right and others I feel like a rookie just starting out! Balancing fairness and individual differences is a big issue for me.

Liz asks whether we are capable of applying the foundational beliefs of our profession to the supervision of staff. How invested are we in our colleagues? Do we have the capacity to nurture consistently the growth and development of others? The issues Liz raises are questions of heart and humanity. How much of each do we have and show? Our roles require that we have substantial amounts of each and that we reveal them on a daily basis.

Martha Sullivan raises similar issues, though in a different way. Martha offers us a style and outlook that reflect the willingness to create space for others to be visible and successful. Such a style requires that we manage our own ego investment in the approaches that staff take and outcomes that they achieve so that the brilliance of others can emerge. If we practice the principle of encouraging openness and honesty within our organization, we will create a context in which members will function as good colleagues to one another and to the senior student affairs officer.

> I like to surround myself with people as strong willed as I am. How else do we have good checks and balances to keep us out of trouble. Yes-people may make us feel good, but in the long run they don't make us look good. If we are dealing with a particular problem in the division, I like to put an idea on the table and all of us attack it. All opinions are valid. Once we arrive at a decision, however, the freewheeling debate is over and we go out as a team. We disagree behind closed doors, sometimes vociferously, but to our constituents we are united.
>
> Do I always succeed in achieving the above? No, certainly not. But it is the atmosphere most of my senior staff and I like to promote. Sometimes newcomers are a bit uncomfortable with our spirited debate but usually come around.
>
> Some of the younger staff members complain that a new president changes his mind. What they don't realize is that someone who really listens, does learn, does change his or her mind. The difficulty in a leadership position is to be open to other ideas without seeming to be wishy-washy. Who ever said inflexibility is a sign of wisdom or strength?
>
> Staff who are mainly process oriented are necessary to keep us all on track. However, they often lose sight of the fact that most administrators are drawn to "can do" mentalities. Why? Because when dealing with a crisis, most of us do not really care who has responsibility for a certain task on the organization chart. All we want to know is who will step up to the plate and get the job done, efficiently, competently, and with a cool head. Often unseasoned professionals feel threatened or uncomfortable in such circumstances when, for whatever reason, they need to step out of the role assigned to them on the organization chart.

Leadership requires that we give structure to the context in which relationships will be developed. We will help members of our organization be clear about what it means to be a team. The senior student affairs officer will offer the most prominent model within the organization of what constitutes openness and care. Leadership for relationship development also demands effective facilitation skills. We must have the ability to lead our organizations through conversations about matters that are important to our institution and our own organization's future. As Martha suggests, it is also important that we have the ability to define a set of parameters to guide conversations and that we are capable of declaring when a conversation is complete.

Martha and Liz each offer insightful perspectives on relationship issues presented to us as supervisors. Jon Dalton looks at relationships in another direction: relationships with bosses. We are often challenged to define how we will relate to and connect with those who supervise us. Such relationships can create tremendous anxiety if we don't have a clear sense of what constitutes a healthy relationship. Because of the power differential between supervisors and employees, many employees will approach their relationship with the supervisor in a tentative and deferential manner. Unfortunately, deference benefits neither the supervisor nor the employee. Such an approach deprives the supervisor of a needed colleague while also extinguishing a perspective that may be crucial to the organization's success on certain issues.

Jon Dalton offers wonderful reflections on his personal journey to acquire the knowledge needed to construct relationships of integrity. Jon offers loyalty as an important value to cultivate in our relationships with bosses. As Jon walks us through his own maturation process he provides a revealing view of the kind of self-critique we must engage in if we are to become more successful in our relationships with others. If we were to practice the same level of self-appraisal modeled by Jon, we would become aware that there are elements of our dealings with others that may not serve us well. Whether it is the manner in which we speak our truth or the standards we use to determine to whom we will accord respect, we all need to work consistently on getting better at how we relate to others. This consistent effort will enhance our capacity to be a good and caring colleague to those with whom we work.

One of the most important relationships in professional life is with one's boss. This relationship is important because it can influence so many aspects of one's professional life—advancement, salary, access to resources, job satisfaction, and professional development. One of the things I learned about this special relationship is how important loyalty is in the routine of professional life and work.

In my younger, more idealistic years, I believed that what bosses wanted most was independent, principled staff who would speak their mind and not be afraid to question authority. I was persuaded that good leaders needed, respected, and rewarded such feedback. In the arrogance of youth I supposed that any leader who didn't prize straight shooters and unpleasant truths was probably not much of a leader anyway. Loyalty was a virtue pretty far down on my scale of professional attributes.

It took me a long time to appreciate the importance of loyalty in my relationships to bosses. Over the course of thirty-five years I've had about eight professional bosses and time enough to think about the meaning of loyalty in different relationships. I did not fully appreciate the importance of loyalty until I became a boss myself and experienced the more complex aspects and responsibilities of leadership. As a young professional I had thought of loyalty as a type of unquestioning obedience and even subservience to another simply because he or she was vested with power. I questioned the value of loyalty because in my way of thinking respect was due someone by the quality of their leadership and character and not simply because they were vested with the power of a position. To give loyalty to someone just because they had a position of power seemed to me to be mere obedience to authority and morally demeaning.

So I actively questioned decisions of bosses that I felt were mistaken and voiced, often in a public way, my concerns about directions or actions I felt were problematic. I tried to convey my opinions in a respectful and positive way but, looking back, I must have often come across as hostile and no doubt arrogant at times.

Through the years I learned that, while bosses almost always respected and promoted me, they often did not take me into their personal confidence. I came to understand that there are times, perhaps much of the time, when what bosses want and need is uncritical support and confirmation. They want and need to have a sense of confidence that their senior leaders will respond in an unconditionally positive way in critical moments when the chips are down. Loyalty means conveying a sense of trust and positive regard that says to bosses that they can count on you and turn to you for support when they need it most.

What I learned as a boss myself, but did not fully appreciate as a young professional, was that loyalty is the glue of friendship between leaders and followers. It does not mean that one gives up independence and principled critique but that one tempers them with a good deal of practical judgment. I learned as a boss that there are many times when what one wants and needs is a sounding board, a receptive and trusted person who will listen and not judge, at least not judge unless requested to do so. Complete loyalty, of course, must ultimately be given only to those one can respect. But I believe loyalty is a virtue that one should practice with all bosses, at least to the point where it cannot be given in good conscience. Leadership can be a lonely business, and loyalty is one of the important ways in which bosses recognize trust and goodwill and build upon it important professional relationships.

Unless we have clear standards for keeping ourselves whole in relationships, we can find ourselves feeling diminished in our relationships with those whom we perceive to have more power than us. Each of us is responsible for making clear to ourselves what we need to do in order to keep our souls intact while we are in relationship with others. At the same time, we need to show the ability to connect with others and be responsive to the needs that they bring to their relationships with us. As Jon points out, unquestioned obedience can carry negative consequences, as can recklessness in our communication. Relationship maturity results in the ability to balance our need to assert an independent perspective with the ability to be loyal to those with whom we are in relationship.

In mutually respectful relationships space is created for the voices of all participants to be heard. Regardless of where we perceive ourselves to be relative to the distribution of power in a relationship, powerful or powerless, each of us of us should work to create space at the center of our relationships for others. All members of our organization have the ability to encourage and embrace or discourage and marginalize. Leaders should represent the standard for what support and encouragement of others look like. As you will note in the following excerpt from Bud Thomas, promoting the growth and success of colleagues is among the most important roles a leader will perform. Bud describes the pride he feels in the success of those with whom he works. Bud's colleagues are able to achieve success because they work within an organizational environment that liberates talented people to utilize their skills and realize their potential.

Bud uses a brief dialogue to cover two important questions concerning relationships. The dialogue approach has embedded within it a number of important lessons relative to developing and managing relationships. As Bud shows through the questions that he offers, leaders must be reflective. Each of us needs a set of recurring questions that we will ask ourselves in order to assess where we are in our relationships with others. The recurring questions will provide us with a sense of grounding. It is important for us to assess whether we are satisfied with our relationships and what those relationships produce for others. How are our care and encouragement of others apparent in our organizations? Are we capable of creating space for others to excel? Are we secure enough to allow attention and acclaim to be directed at others? While these questions may seem simple they are not.

There are leaders who are not secure enough to create space for the talents of others to emerge. Such leaders need to be the focus of attention in their organization and use their power to keep others in a position where they cannot shine too brightly. Emotionally secure leaders are able to share credit concerning the success of the organization. They also use language to describe the success of the organization that is reflective of their honoring the contributions of their colleagues. My personal observation is that the leaders who are most insecure describe the success of the organization with reference to "I" and "my." Inclusive leaders view success through the lens of "we" and "our." As Bud's response suggests, when we construct encouraging and caring relationships with our colleagues we cannot take credit for the success they achieve, but we can feel a sense of pride at being somehow connected to that success.

Q: What have been the points of satisfaction?

BUD: I ask that question of a lot of people who have come for interviews over the years. What have you done that you're most proud of? The most significant thing, in my judgment, is that the university has a good reputation in student affairs work and in higher education. I'm very proud of the fact that a whole bunch of our people have been nationally recognized and are leaders in their areas of expertise. I feel a sense of pride in large measure because I know that without a solid home base, they couldn't have done that, so having that home base that I have had a hand in managing. . ., I'm proud of that. I'm also proud that we run a very good set of programs, and our students are enriched as they go through here. As best as we can tell, based on what little data we have to work with, and we don't have anywhere as much as we need, we help them . . ., or at *least* we don't do them much damage. I believe we're good at both helping and doing no harm. Our people know what they are doing, and our people are effectively connected with whatever their science is. That's their business and they're pretty much at the top of their game. As a result of that, as they do their work well, students are getting the best that our group thinking and talents have to offer. So, that's probably the best we can do with student development, and that's a source of great pride.

I also am personally very proud of the people I worked with. I get a rush of pride when I see an individual do well that I have some reason to believe I had something to do with. Other things contribute to success of course, but there is a relationship between the talents of the people who have performed well and the enabling and supporting environments that we have managed to keep intact. Performance requirements are a function of the pressures that occur, mostly from people. Issues and incidents that come up are interpreted quickly by people, and put into action on the scene . . ., in the environment . . ., through the eyes and the psychological screening system of the people at work. So the people essentially determine whatever happens. We've been able for a long period of time to manage to keep an environment that is supportive and that has been created for people to work in optimally. I guess that the environment and the people are at the core of the things that I've viewed as the most significant of my participation.

Q: What kind of instincts do you use toward people?

BUD: Well, *instincts* is a great word; I use the word a lot, and I believe it describes a phenomenon that we all have. It's a combination of experience, wisdom, and juices. But it doesn't always work. I used to say that my first-impression assessment of people was about 50 percent accurate. That's only raw chance. So instincts alone in those particular encounters didn't get me very far. In most judgments, you have to go beyond first impressions, get additional data, and then develop informed and more valid impressions over time.

As Bud suggests, instincts are an important part of our interactions with others. Sometimes those instincts will serve us well; other times they will lead us astray. The important thing to note about the use of instincts is the fact that at times we will rely upon our gut feelings and instincts about people and situations. Leaders are challenged to manage reliance upon their instincts in relation to the instincts of others when faced with making decisions where no clear-cut answer is apparent. Successful leaders will have examples of organizational decisions that have been driven by the instincts of others and in which the inclination of the leader differs from the final outcome.

Linda Riesser offers insight on the range of work environments in which she has worked—work climates that ranged from toxic to deeply collaborative. In each environment there was an emotional tone that was maintained by members. The most important message in Linda's writing is that the climates in those organizations did not happen by accident, particularly the positive environments. Implicitly or explicitly we lead our organization in a particular direction. Isolation of the leader influences isolation within the organization. However, engagement by leaders models and communicates openness to others.

Linda points out the importance of simple courtesies: respecting others, showing appreciation for their work, and offering thanks. She offers that we must create opportunities to celebrate, laugh together, and be playful. As leaders we are capable of using our roles to allow the humanity of our organizations to show.

At the 2001 NASPA conference, I attended a session on transformational leadership and was impressed by the findings that they rely heavily on relationships to get things done. They "seed conversations with values," and they sense when the time is right for initiatives. I have found the quality of relationships and communication to be incredibly important in how I feel about the workplace, and it does have a huge impact on what gets accomplished. I have worked in places where there was tension, competition, old grudges, and mutual dislike. Those were the most toxic.

I have also worked in settings where most staff interacted politely with a fairly small number of colleagues, functioning in departmental silos without much personal relating or connection to others. The best places involved people who worked hard but laughed often, who supported and enjoyed each other, who were mobilized to work toward the same priorities, and who felt part of a larger community.

Those nurturing and inclusive places do not happen by accident. I believe they can be created and maintained through conscious efforts to build trust, address morale problems, energize with excitement and vision, and celebrate regularly. Again, the leader's influence is vital. It is hard to balance the "high team" and "high task" aspects of the job. I could easily sit at my desk all day, absorbed in projects, e-mail, and memos. I have had to remind myself to spend quality time with students and staff and to include time to listen to them, find out who they are as persons, and be empathic and appreciative, rather than strictly task-oriented. As I have moved to new jobs, I have reminded myself that what has remained meaningful from past positions is not the paper processed and problems solved but the people I worked with and the lasting changes in students. So I have visited every person in the division in his or her office and tried to understand what they do, how they feel, and what they would like to change.

I have tried also to attend all kinds of campus events and to look for opportunities to acknowledge the contributions of those behind the scenes. I continue to remember a staff member who kept a Post-it note on her refrigerator for months. It was one sentence of praise from the president. Those little acknowledgements let people know that their work is never taken for granted. I see committee work as an opportunity to network across departments. I have become more committed to retreats, potlucks, and after-work get-togethers, especially if they involve interactive time, creative projects, food, conversation, and music. I have found that no kick-off in-service session, retirement, or funny incident should go by without a humorous song, poem, gag gift, or satirical tribute. The informal connections and celebrations are invisible forces fostering a supportive community.

On the job, my relationship with my supervisor is extremely important. I have adapted to many different styles and valued the people who were accessible, genuine, and reliable in helping me get the resources or the decisions I needed. I tend to be a self-directed worker, with a voluminous "to do" list. On it, I list things to report and consult about, so the precious time with the chief executive officer is used well. Sometimes the best time to sit and "debrief" is after 5:00 P.M., when we are both working late. I want to know that we have the same priorities. Supervisors are often so busy with their own priorities that they lose sight of what I am working on, don't know what I need them to do, or assume that I know what their highest priorities are. So it's important to report regularly, ask for support, and clarify expectations. I also appreciate it when they reinforce equality and partnership between the dean of instruction and me, although I try to put regular energy into meeting with my counterpart and launching joint projects. I also revere supervisors who understand the profession called student development, and the theory and research associated with it. If they don't, I look for any opportunity to gently educate. Again, I have found that intangible trust factor to be critical.

On a personal level, I think it's critical to find kindred spirits outside of our jobs with whom we can vent, be ourselves, and share renewal time. We spend so much energy in service to others or to the institution, and we must choose our words in those leadership roles. I have come to treasure friends who are conscious communicators, that is, they are skilled at listening, asking questions, paraphrasing, and helping me find the best solution or the personal learning. They allow me the luxury of candid self-disclosure and offer it in return. They are fully present. They reflect from many perspectives (for example, theoretically, politically, metaphorically). I have learned to put more time into those relationships that are truly reciprocal and growth-supporting, with people who are also committed to larger causes, creative projects, and/or personal development. They are like gold.

Linda offers excellent guidance for how we can construct positive relations in an organization. She acknowledges the learning that she carries with her as she has moved through her professional life. With each new position we are challenged to reflect our accumulated knowledge and increased sophistication in how we manage relationships and situations. The following perspective looks at relationship management throughout the life span of our relationship with an organization—from time of application to interview to job offer to acceptance and arrival to time of departure from the organization. Too often when we think about developing and managing relationships we neglect to think about the earliest and final stage of the relationship. The ensuing reflection piece offers my own thoughts on aspects of our relationships with organizations that we often overlook.

Often when we think about constructing and maintaining positive work relationships we focus on the relationships in which we find ourselves engaged on a day-to-day basis. However, I have found that the context for our relationships is set from the time that we first interact with a prospective employer. Too few of us pay close attention to the quality of the way that we enter organizations and the way that we leave organizations.

I believe that from the time that I write a letter of application or respond to a call from an institution that is recruiting me, I am in a relationship with that institution. All of my subsequent behaviors should be guided by the thought that I need to treat this relationship as if it is one that matters to me. Every mismanaged conversation or unpleasant interaction becomes a hurdle that will ultimately need to be cleared if I find myself working at the institution. I have made it a habit to try to interact with members of the institution in a manner that suggests that I regard them as colleagues from the earliest communication. I believe it is important for me to get a sense of the tone of the organization and introduce the organization to my way of being as soon as possible. I have observed many candidates mismanage their relationship with a prospective institution by being rude to or difficult in their dealings with office support staff while making arrangements for the campus interview. These interactions often get communicated to others on the campus and even if the person prevails as the successful candidate the behaviors remain in the institutional memory.

Interviews provide the first opportunity for solid relationship grounding with a number of different people. It is important to manage those interactions as if you are constructing a network of relationships that you will bear responsibility for sustaining. I make it a habit to not say anything in an interview conversation that I am not willing to be held accountable for should I accept the position. I pay a great deal of attention to how I come into an organization. When negotiating salary and other conditions, I do so with the recognition that I will need to be in a significant relationship with the person with whom I am negotiating. I am conscious of leaving the conversation at a level that will not require repair in order for the relationship to be successful. Relationships can be compromised and corrupted in the name of fighting for what you think you deserve. When I enter a new organization I am cognizant of the impact that my words have. I focus more on becoming attuned to the dominant conversation occurring within the organization than I am with making my voice heard. It is more important for me to enter into and enhance the existing relationship network than it is to construct a relationship network around me. Listening to others is the most successful way I have found to form positive relationships with others. I try to be careful how much I talk, how boldly I proclaim, and how publicly I make judgments. I have found it virtually impossible to successfully lead an organization from outside the relationship structures. I believe strongly that you must "live" in the organization if you hope to effectively lead the organization.

While there tends to be thoughtfulness given to how we enter organizations, we often depart with much greater impulsiveness. I have observed a number of excellent leaders undo their positive reputations and legacies by leaving organizations thoughtlessly. The typical way we do ourselves harm is "firing a few last shots." Too often the shots that are fired hit the wrong people. I believe it is as important for us to manage our relationships positively as we leave an organization as it is to manage them well as we enter. When we depart an organization we should leave every relationship at a level that we could return to it with no regrets and no shame about how we have been or what we have said.

Peggy Barr reflects on the theme of departing organizations as she shares a story about a retirement dinner that she attended at which a valued colleague was honored. The story Peggy relates shows the value of being gracious and respectful in our treatment of others. She suggests that legacies are constructed from our day-to-day interactions—the opportunities that we have to show our kindness and our willingness to believe in others. The powerful stories that Peggy conveys offer a simple and poignant message—our relationships are our legacy.

This spring I attended a banquet in honor of a dean who was retiring after twenty-five years of service to the university, the business community, and his students. It was a grand affair (I bet if you counted the net worth of those who came to honor him it would have been in the billions of dollars). I was struck, however, by the simple acts of kindness that people recalled about his work. Almost in passing, people discussed his many and innovative achievements and the remarkable ranking of the business school under his leadership. But it was the acts of kindness, of caring, of commitment that moved so many to be there and to honor him. That was why I was there. He was one of the first to greet me when I came on the campus. He became a partner with the division of student affairs on a number of projects, including helping our career center, although his focus was solely on graduate business students.

He provided financial support for projects. But most of all he cared, valued excellence, and was supportive of hard work and commitment. He taught me a lot, although he was known as a curmudgeon to some (for he did not suffer fools gladly). To me he was a friend and partner.

That lovely evening caused me to reflect on the relationships that we develop and the power that they have to be life transforming in others and in ourselves. It is the core of what we do in student affairs—helping people grow and develop to their full potential. And it is good work to have done and to be doing.

Earlier this year I received an e-mail from a student who had been excluded from the university for repeated violations of our drug policy. When he left he was angry, blaming everyone but himself and absolutely knew that I was out to get him. It was not a pleasant interaction for either of us. When he left I gave him a letter that indicated that if he got treatment and stayed clean I would release his transcripts so that he could complete his college education at another institution. Three years after he was excluded he wrote and provided documentation of a successful drug treatment program, his transcripts were released, and he enrolled in another institution. I did not hear from him again until last fall when he tracked me down after he learned of my retirement. He wrote to thank me for holding him accountable, for saying no, for offering him an option to turn his life around but being firm with him at the same time. He told me I was the first person in his life who had said no and meant it. And while he did not understand it at the time he grew to appreciate the care that went into that decision and wanted to let me know that. He finished college and is working on an advanced degree while working full time. He made my day!

Relationships with students are those that take both time and patience. Bill Monat, my former president at Northern Illinois University, used to say that he expected a vice president for student affairs (or for that matter any student affairs professional) to "speak up for students but never down to them." This does not mean that we always agree or that we condone unacceptable behavior but it does mean that we are respectful in our interactions with them and in the process teach them a valuable lesson—one we hope goes with them as they leave the institution.

The same can be said for our colleagues both within and without the division of student affairs. Listening carefully and treating them with respect should be a hallmark of our professional practice (although at times it is not easy to do so). I commend Art Sandeen's chapter on building relationships in *The Handbook of Student Affairs Administration* (Barr and others, 2000) to you for some helpful guidance and suggestions on this most difficult of issues. Simple acts of kindness make a difference, as do gestures of appreciation. Jim Rhatigan set a model for us all on developing relationships as he and members of his staff reached out to new faculty on the Wichita State campus. Notes of appreciation, remembering special occasions, and reaching out at times of stress make a huge difference in how people feel about themselves and about how they fit into the organization. Aretha Franklin had it right when she sang R-E-S-P-E-C-T, for that is what all of us want and need. There is something to learn from almost everyone, and the lessons can often be life altering.

I used to tell my colleagues that those of us who work in student affairs are teachers and that our classroom is just different than those of our academic colleagues. For we teach in everything that we do. Students and staff members learn from us in both intentional and unintentional ways. How we handle conflict, good news, bad news, behavioral problems, and our daily interactions with them may make a profound difference in their lives and how they will handle those same issues in the future.

Finally, it goes without saying that we must demonstrate integrity in our relationships both on and off the campus and be truth tellers. We should make no promises that we cannot deliver, and we should deliver what we promise. If those simple guidelines are followed then all of our relationships will flourish and prosper.

All relationships have a life span—some last throughout the duration of our professional life; others are as brief as a onetime interaction. Regardless of length every relationship deserves to be treated as important. The briefest interaction, dealing with what appears to be the most mundane issue, can have a tremendous impact on the person to whom that issue matters most. Our role requires that we be as present in our conversations about what appears to be trivial as we are in conversations dealing with issues to which large numbers of people attach great importance. Our work should be guided by the belief that all people and all conversations matter. If we approach our relationships with graciousness, openness, and humility we will put ourselves in the position to honor the humanity and gifts that others bring to us. As educators and leaders no outcome is more important for us to achieve in our relationships with others than to recognize, cultivate, and encourage the gifts of those with whom we lead, learn, and collaborate.

Reference

Barr, M. J., and others. *The Handbook of Student Affairs Administration* (2nd ed.). San Francisco: Jossey-Bass, 2000.

LARRY ROPER *is the vice provost for student affairs and professor of ethnic studies at Oregon State University and an adjunct faculty member in the College Student Services Administration Program, where he teaches and serves as an academic advisor. He serves as editor for the* NASPA Journal.

3

This chapter examines the career paths of student affairs leaders and their reflections on the factors that matter most in making important career choices.

Reflections on Career Development Among Student Affairs Leaders

Gregory S. Blimling

Children do not dream about becoming a senior student affairs officer (SSAO), nor is it part of the conversation about career options among junior high school or high school students. Unlike becoming a doctor, lawyer, firefighter, or even a politician, work in student affairs is not a commonly discussed career option. I am not aware of any undergraduate programs devoted specifically to educating student affairs administrators. Most students are introduced to a career in student affairs through their contact with student affairs professionals they meet through their co-curricular undergraduate work. It is not really until graduate school that this area of specialization emerges as a career option. Peggy Barr explained her entrance into the field in this way: "No one grows up saying they want to be a dean of students or vice president for student affairs. It was not until I was in college and got involved in student activities that I realized that people actually got paid for doing this type of work! What a wonderful revelation! And what wonderful people they were to encourage me and help me see possibilities beyond being a fifth-grade teacher."

What career path leads student affairs professionals through the field, and how do people find themselves in positions as SSAOs? These are some of the questions that were addressed in a series of reflections and personal logs that a group of SSAOs considered during the past year. In this chapter, I will summarize some of their observations and isolate some of the factors that have led this group of SSAOs to the positions they either now hold or recently held, what they have done to manage their careers, how they balanced their personal and professional lives, and why they stayed or left their SSAO positions. I will include some observations about contributions they felt they were able to make in their positions that were fulfilling to them personally and which contributed meaningfully to the education of students on their individual campuses. Finally, I will offer some conclusions that emerged from among this group of SSAOs.

Multiple Career Paths

It is not a secret that most people enter student affairs work because of student leadership positions they held as undergraduates and because of relationships they establish with student affairs professionals who supported them as undergraduates. Work as a resident assistant, fraternity or sorority leader, student union board leader, or leader in student government is a common path into student affairs work. After completing master's level graduate work, the most common entry points are in residence life, fraternity and sorority advising, and work in student activities. None of the SSAOs who contributed to this chapter started their careers in higher education expecting to be an SSAO. For most, their careers seemed to emerge without much intentional planning.

Peggy Barr describes it this way: "I had a series of increasingly responsible jobs in three different institutions and enjoyed them. I enjoyed my colleagues, and even though this was the era of student protests, I enjoyed students. . . . I knew I had a career when I realized I could not imagine working in any other environment and that I probably was going to do this work the rest of my professional life. It was then I decided to go back to school to shape the environments I would be working in during the rest of my life."

When I started in student affairs work, I never planned to be a vice chancellor. I was happy doing what I was doing. When I recognized that I could do my supervisor's job as well as that person was doing it, I began thinking of myself in that role and throughout my career was either promoted at the institution at which I was working or I was given opportunities at other institutions. I didn't really manage my career as much as I pursued opportunities after the job I was currently doing no longer offered me the interest and challenge it did when I started.

The talents, skills, and interests of the SSAOs presented them with opportunities. Others recognized qualities in them and offered them increased responsibilities. Some of the SSAOs came from nontraditional student affairs backgrounds and believed that the things they learned in other roles in higher education gave them a different perspective on student affairs work and a different vantage point on the field. Doris Ching came from a position as a faculty member and writes: "I am confident in my observation that a diversity of academic preparation in professional backgrounds in student affairs and academic affairs strengthens the student affairs staff and leads to better communication, greater collaboration, and higher respect for faculty in the schools, colleges, and academic departments; on the other hand (as a former faculty member), I have a strong desire to do right by my student affairs colleagues."

Careers are not random. People make choices and can manage their careers. Larry Roper emphasized this need: "When you manage your career, you are responsible for making clear the conditions of your employment. The ideal is to choose to work only at an institution that is consistent with your values and beliefs. . . . If you are to manage your career responsibly, nobody should ever take your goals and aspirations more seriously than you. Consistent with that, you should always be in control of when you leave the institution."

None of the SSAOs outlined a specific track that would lead to a vice chancellor or vice president's position. In all cases, the SSAOs believed that it was a combination of opportunities, skills, good fortune, and hard work. Although one can, to some extent, manage the movement among various positions that are more likely than not to lead to a SSAO position, a variety of circumstances can intervene in the best-laid plans. Family responsibilities, dual-career marriages, institutional changes, and a variety of personal and economic circumstances combine to form a tension between opportunities for advancement and a desire to remain at an institution in a position from which one still derives satisfaction. No one suggested that becoming an SSAO should be a career goal for anyone. To the contrary, people have found success in their careers by contributing in a variety of ways, and the notion that leading a division of student affairs should be a goal for professionals in student affairs was not embraced by any of the SSAOs.

Art Sandeen and Charles Schroeder commented about the importance of engaging in new academic work, writing, studying, and working to keep ahead of new approaches being advanced in student affairs. They did this to avoid stagnation and to do the best job possible. But this commitment also prepared them to gain opportunities for advancement and to successfully maintain positions of significant responsibility. Art Sandeen writes:

> My immigrant grandfather was a carpenter and he told me once that when a new tool came on the market, he knew he had to buy it if he was going to remain competitive in his profession. I tried to follow this same path in my career; I knew I had to read, to study, and to consider new ideas all the time if I was going to survive as a leader. I felt this was only my responsibility—not that of my institution or my professional association. I learned a great deal from my colleagues, of course, but my continual learning was primarily my own job and it was a lifelong pursuit.

Charles Schroeder writes: "Finally, I have avoided a sense of stagnation by engaging in continuous learning activities. These have come primarily through a range of professional activities—research, writing, presentations, consulting, leadership roles in the American College Personnel Association

(ACPA), and other associations. Because I need a high degree of stimulation, I have always championed two or three major projects on an annual basis. These, among other activities, have kept me energized, productive, focused, and fulfilled."

Balance Between Career and Personal Life

Being an SSAO usually means an administrative life filled with meetings, problems, institutional issues, student crises, and a full calendar of social events ranging from those initiated by students to those required by trustees and the president. No SSAO indicated that the position did not offer sufficient challenge or that the job left them with too much free time. Instead, the issues concerned how one learns to balance the demands of the position with one's personal life. Typical of the responses from SSAOs was Charles Schroeder's: "As important as my work and professional commitments have been, I have always placed my family first. In this regard, I never missed any of my son's high school football, basketball, or baseball games and always attended all of my daughter's social and athletic events. Similarly, I have always been renewed by a variety of adventure-oriented activities—downhill skiing, rock climbing, sky diving, hunting, backpacking, and various trips throughout the world."

It is easy for SSAOs to think that who they are is the same as what they do. SSAOs are "on stage" so often that it can be difficult for them to set aside the role and recognize that they have personal needs and an identity outside their position. Art Sandeen explains: "Among the most important things I tried to learn was that I was not my job. I tried not to define myself or my life in terms of my job and tried to develop a strong sense of personal identity that was not dependent on having any job. I loved my work, but I was convinced I would be the same person regardless of the job I might have in life."

Decision to Stay or Move to a New Institution as an SSAO

By far the greatest number of comments concerned decisions about staying in a position as an SSAO at an institution or moving to pursue opportunities at a different institution as an SSAO or as a college president. I think that SSAOs struggle with this issue occasionally because universities are often in a state of change, with relatively frequent turnover in presidents and other administrative officers. Unfortunately, the student affairs profession has encouraged the idea that to advance in the field, one needs to change institutions. Some of this may be the reality of working at an institution where opportunities to move may be limited by specialization within the institution and the longevity of people holding positions to which one is most likely to advance. Regardless, changing positions is something that SSAOs consider at various times in their career, as do most people.

One of the interesting characteristics of the group of SSAOs who contributed to this chapter is that about half have stayed at their institution for most of their career and about half changed jobs, in some cases holding several positions as an SSAO at different institutions. Bud Thomas believed that staying at an institution was a necessary commitment to an institution. He writes: "So when we have people that come through in significant positions that leave too quickly, there is either a mistake in hiring or they're making a mistake. We each ought to invest seriously when doing our kind of work, even though ultimately we have to make judgments according to our own best interests. We put graduate students in entry-level positions expecting them to move, but even they ought to have a commitment to that job, while they are in it, as though they are never going to leave!"

SSAOs pointed to several factors that contributed to decisions to leave a university. One of these factors was recognition that the institution or organization at which they were working needed a different kind of leadership. Liz Nuss describes her decision to leave her leadership position at NASPA: "After eight years it was increasingly apparent that the organization needed to be launched to the next level. It needed someone who was enthusiastic and skilled in grantsmanship and who had a more entrepreneurial approach. Those were not the things I liked to do, nor was I the best at those tasks. I concluded it was time for change for me and the association."

A similar response comes from Peggy Barr, who had developed a good understanding of her leadership strengths and the kind of circumstances in which she could be most useful to her university. She writes:

> I have learned that I am not a good program maintainer—that is why I have been a vice president at three different institutions. I'm good at diagnosing problems and creating teams and helping people grow and develop. I have learned that I have skill in reorganizing functions and services. I also know that once that has happened I start to fix things that are not broken—and that isn't good for me, my colleagues, or the organization. . . . I admire folks like Bud (William) Thomas and Art Sandeen who stayed at one institution and hung in there through thick and thin, but my skills are different and that is OK.

Having a clear understanding of what your strengths and weaknesses are contributes to decisions about where you can be most effective. But this is not always an easy determination. As Liz Nuss explained it: "It is difficult to accurately assess whether one's leadership style is appropriate for the current challenges an institution or organization faces. In some organizations it is possible for the leader to be versatile and facile. In others, the leader has considerable flexibility in selecting assistants and can bring new perspectives and skills on the team. But in some organizations it is important for the leaders to recognize when they need to be replaced so that the best leadership skills are available."

If one looks only at one's skills and what the institution needs, SSAOs could change as quickly as the institutional climate changes. But the SSAO is often not alone in the decision making. A spouse, children, family, and friends influence this decision. At a stage in one's career, there often is an interest in settling into a community and developing stable, long-lasting relationships. Opportunities that exist are weighed against a variety of criteria. More money being offered at another university may be a consideration, but Larry Roper warns: "Don't just follow the money. The choices I made early in my career were related more to following opportunities. Avoid getting trapped in a job because of money. This is the most difficult temptation to avoid."

Decisions about staying or leaving are complex. They not only involve one's skills, personal commitments, and financial issues but also involve relationships established at a particular institution. Does the president of the institution support student affairs? Does the vice president for student affairs have a good relationship with other vice presidents, the trustees, and various student groups at the institution? Does the vice president have the support he or she needs from staff? Is the budget adequate to support the programs in student affairs and is the environment one in which one feels fulfilled by the responsibilities? All of these are questions that SSAOs and other people in student affairs wrestle with in making the decision about staying, leaving, or returning. Typical of the importance shown to personal relationships at an institution are the comments of Linda Reisser, who wrote: "I keep learning how important the leader is and to keep my life boat ready. I want to feel part of a committed, innovative team in a caring, positive community. I watched some place-bound colleagues get stagnant or cynical when the institution moved in a different direction. Being single, it was easier for me to be mobile."

Sometimes ethical issues are a consideration in whether or not to remain at an institution. Occasionally, other decision makers at an institution make judgments that are antithetical to the best interest of students, in opposition to commitments that were made, and in some cases unethical. I would like to believe that this happens infrequently, but I have been in higher education long enough to know that it does happen. When confronted by a situation like this, SSAOs must decide how to respond, when to respond, when not to respond, and how much they are willing personally to risk in that response. Ethical concerns present serious career conflicts for SSAOs. If a person offers to resign a position because of a decision, it cannot be a threat. It is not something a person does lightly, and the person must be prepared to leave. This is usually a "last resort" effort, reserved for the most extreme situations. Because leadership across higher education is uneven and fluid, heavily influenced by financial and political events, ethical conflicts do emerge. Charles Schroeder explained the influence of ethical issues on his career in this way: "In my career I can think of at least five occasions where I put my job on the line—in three instances on behalf of staff members and in the other two based on principled positions that I took with regard to critical campus life issues. In one case, I actually lost my position based on the principled approach that I maintained."

Several of the SSAOs commented on the need to have an "exit strategy" so that when the time came—by their choice, the choice of a new president, ethical circumstances, or other issues—they had a plan on what to do after being an SSAO. Although career counselors spend a considerable amount of time telling undergraduate students that they develop functionally transferable skills by majoring in history or English and can get a job in a variety of different fields, after a significant career in student affairs, a transition to a position outside of higher education seems remote. Yes, SSAOs develop a variety of skills and some do move to positions outside of higher education. But by far most SSAOs consider an exit strategy within higher education. This might be working with one of the national student affairs associations, developing a consulting relationship in some specialized area of expertise such as leadership training, or moving into a different area of the university such as fundraising or athletics. However, the most frequent consideration has been to move from the SSAO position into a faculty position teaching student affairs, higher education, or a closely related field.

At one time it was customary for SSAOs to receive some type of faculty appointment and tenure. Few institutions still offer this contractual opportunity at the time of employment. SSAOs with the requisite academic credentials, skills, and research experience can earn faculty positions and often successfully meet the academic requirements to be tenured as faculty members. Even those who have not been able to arrange for a formal relationship frequently find opportunities after leaving their SSAO position to join with faculty colleagues and share their administrative experience in student affairs with graduate students studying in higher education and college student affairs.

For many of the SSAOs who contributed to this study, there has been an internal struggle between the desire to lead a division of student affairs and the desire to teach in a student affairs program. With few exceptions, the SSAOs who were invited to participate in this volume were asked because their visibility in the student affairs field was gained through a combination of administrative success and significant contributions to the research and literature in student affairs. It is not possible to conclude that this would be true of other SSAOs who have not chosen to invest themselves in these two dimensions of student affairs work.

Typical of the dilemma faced by SSAOs who have struggled with having one foot in the classroom and one foot in the boardroom is Art Sandeen's comments:

I'm pleased that I made my planned transition to the faculty (from the vice president's position) and that I was able to do it on my terms, at a time when my work was viewed positively by my colleagues in student affairs and administration. I have witnessed too many friends and colleagues who have been forced out of their senior student affairs positions and with the politics of institutions being so volatile these days, I was fortunate to make my move when I did. It is always best, if possible, to move when one is still wanted.

The only irritating aspect of my current role is that some colleagues assume I have essentially retired and am just coasting for a few years until I formally retire! I suspect my old Calvinist background causes me to become defensive about any suggestion that I am taking it easy! After thirty-eight years of rigorous work and long hours each day and night, I've found such habits impossible to break. I now seem to work almost the same hours I did before! I guess we are who we are!

Not everyone who has moved from an SSAO position to a faculty position has settled on this dimension of his or her career. Occasionally, an SSAO may leave this position only to have second thoughts after entering the faculty ranks. The internal conflict does not necessarily change, just the position one holds and the responsibilities at that time. Linda Reisser explains it as follows: "I started to look at another career move. Should I stay in teaching or get back on the administrative track? This has been an ongoing conflict, and I've found it very hard to combine the scholar role with the practitioner role. It's so hard to read, let alone write, when you're working sixty hours a week on multiple tasking. Nevertheless, I miss being in charge of staff and resources that could affect larger numbers of students."

Finally, some SSAOs think about teaching at some stage in their career. Although they have not made the decision, they continue to contemplate the issue. Like many other SSAOs, I have thought about teaching full-time. I hold a tenured faculty position, and when my administrative life gets particularly stressful, I occasionally think about moving to the classroom. I have tried to remain actively engaged in scholarship in the field, and I teach one course a year. I suspect that someday I will teach full-time. But for now, I still enjoy creating new programs and working with a great staff in their efforts to promote student learning on our campus.

What about receiving a promotion beyond the SSAO position, such as becoming the president of an institution? Some SSAOs have considered this move, and some SSAOs do leave student affairs and become college presidents. Higher education can create barriers to this transition. Bud Thomas explains his decision this way: "At a couple of points in my career, I was encouraged to try to become a president . . . and I was nominated for a few different places. It is my observation that a degree in higher education administration is not what would, on its face, license you to become a president of a major university or other very good college. You can do it, but it is not likely. There is a litmus test of getting by a faculty-dominated screening committee that is very difficult."

For the most part, SSAOs who contributed to this chapter enjoyed what they were doing and moved to other student affairs positions rather than to positions as a president of a university. For other SSAOs, being close to seeing what a university president really does was enough to dissuade them from pursuing that career option. Social demands, fundraising, and political considerations imposed on university presidents can be a deterrent for some SSAOs who might otherwise consider pursuing such a position.

Staying in the position as an SSAO requires a commitment to students. Several SSAOs commented about their relationship with students as one of the most important aspects of being a good SSAO. SSAOs usually spend less time with students and more time with other student affairs administrators who work with students. Two SSAOs commented on how their relationship with students sustained them throughout their career and made their commitment to remaining an SSAO important to them. Charles Schroeder writes: "As a vice chancellor, I also found tremendous amounts of fulfillment in working formally and informally with students. I would always designate Wednesday afternoons as my 'walk about time'—that is, leaving the office and 'dropping in' on students throughout the campus. I also relished opportunities to host student dinners at my home—I often learned much more from students about the quality of their experience (or lack of) than I did from my staff."

Commenting about his relationship with students Art Sandeen writes: "As I assess my administrative career, I'm glad I made the effort to spend a lot of time with individual students; it gave me great joy, and now I wish I had done even more of it! While I am also glad I spent considerable time reading and writing, I know that my emotions and feelings drove my work more than my intellect or mind. Student affairs work is not very cerebral; it is mainly about passion!"

Observations and Conclusions

Gathering information in a nonstructured way from selected SSAOs is not a method designed to represent a consensus of judgment on how SSAOs regard the position. Comments from the people who contributed to this book are reflections of their individual experiences, likes, dislikes, idiosyncrasies, and personal life issues. Each is a story of success and fulfillment in their contributions to student affairs in their role as an SSAO.

Despite the highly individual experiences and observations made by the group of contributors, several themes emerge from their reflections. First is a dedication to students in doing the best they can on behalf of students. One SSAO referred to it as a "passion." Another referred to it as offering him a "tremendous amount of fulfillment." Although no one specifically described working with students as the reason they entered student affairs work, all of the SSAOs defined the success in their careers in terms of accomplishments that helped students.

A second theme that emerges from these reports is the struggle that many of the SSAOs wrestled with about staying in the position or moving to another position. I suspect that this internal struggle reflects in part the political nature of administrative roles in complex organizations. It is easy to make a mistake; and in an age when accountability and fault-finding are often equated, it is easy for others to judge administrators accordingly. The longevity of college presidents and vice presidents in the same administrative position has decreased over time, and it is increasingly difficult to find people who have the experience necessary to assume these positions. For these and other reasons, SSAOs advised the need for an "exit strategy." Again, this issue is related to staying in the position or choosing another position. But the exit strategy usually concerns what to do after the SSAO position, how to make the transition, how to announce it to staff and others, and when to do it.

Related to this concern has been the struggle that many of the SSAOs had with how they could best make their contribution in higher education. This issue focused on either staying as an administrator or becoming a faculty member. Those who made the transition to being a faculty member generally reported that they were very fulfilled by the new responsibilities. Some reported that they were still uncertain as to whether they had made the right decision.

Finally, SSAOs commonly addressed the issue of balance in their lives. Some regretted not having had better balance between family life and the responsibilities of their job. Others felt they had made a responsible commitment to their family as their first priority and to themselves in addition to successfully fulfilling the expectations of their position. Perhaps the best advice offered to SSAOs thinking about career issues is from Charles Schroeder: "I realize now, more than ever, that life is not a dress rehearsal—this is it! Hence, I am devoting more and more of my discretionary time to a series of daily and weekly activities that provide deeper meaning for my life."

GREGORY BLIMLING *is vice chancellor for student development at Appalachian State University. He serves as editor of the* Journal of College Student Development, *published by the American College Personnel Association.*

4

Managing change is one of the most complex skills of leadership. This chapter examines some of the most difficult changes confronted by student affairs leaders and the practical wisdom they have gained from these encounters.

Managing Change in Student Affairs Leadership Roles

Jon C. Dalton, Diana Imanuel Gardner

In *Who Moved My Cheese?* (Spencer, 1998), the little mouse characters learn faster than the little people that the "cheese" of success is always moving and that one must be flexible and constantly ready for change in its pursuit. Although this modern parable celebrates change it also has a dark side. Change is portrayed as random and chaotic interventions that require individuals to live in fear of the loss of achievement and security and to continually make new beginnings. It is an image of change that touches some of our deepest fears about managing the challenges of life and work.

Some changes are transforming and have lasting impact. They can completely reorient the nature of what we do so that we are forced to think and act in radically new and different ways in order to adjust to fast-moving forces. The impact of computer technology on the processes of higher education is an example of transforming change. We should be cautious, however, about using transforming changes as paradigms for all change. Truly transforming changes are quite rare in the run of things. For example, as fast as applied computer technology has been incorporated into student affairs applications, the changes have not occurred overnight. The information revolution has not so much stormed across the landscape of our work as it has been a relentless tide that has slowly eroded the old landscape and shaped a new one.

Most of the changes routinely encountered in the professional work of student affairs are not transforming in nature and can be anticipated with good planning and by staying vigilant to emerging trends and innovations. We have witnessed, for example, numerous organizational and management reforms come and go in higher education over the last two decades, many of which were imported from the corporate sector. They created much

NEW DIRECTIONS FOR STUDENT SERVICES, no. 98, Summer 2002 © Wiley Periodicals, Inc.

sound and fury and had their day, but in the end their impact was usually not lasting or transforming. Seasoned administrators know how to ride out these occasional shake-ups.

The fact that most changes come gradually, sometimes almost imperceptibly, however, can lull us into thinking that they are of little consequence. Herein lies the challenge of managing change—to learn to detect the long-term transforming potential that is embedded in the ordinary changes and developments that come to us day in and out. Perhaps the most difficult aspect of managing change comes from within, from our own human inclinations to become too comfortable with customary and familiar things.

Change should be neither feared nor worshipped. Managing change is an important and essential aspect of professional leadership, but it is not an elusive science. The tools and strategies for dealing with change are much the same as those used for other complex, long-range planning activities. We will review some of these changes as well as strategies for addressing them later in this chapter. It is important to try to demystify some of the popular claims about change because there is often too much adulation of change for its own sake and too much emphasis on change as inherently complex. It is important to keep in mind when dealing with change issues that many of those who are such zealots for particular changes are often motivated by proprietary interests or influenced by ideological biases. Proposals for changes so often seem to come wrapped in passionate visions and a sales pitch.

The Difference Between Enduring Change Versus Fads and Fashion

If it is important to recognize and respond to significant changes that alter the nature of our work, it is equally important to avoid the pursuit of every new trend, fad, fashion, and gimmick that purports to be trend-setting and revolutionary. Pursuing change for change's sake wastes much time and enormous resources. Much of what is touted as "new" is neither novel nor significant. One must be able to separate the changes and developments that will significantly affect the mission and work of student affairs, either immediately or over time, from those that claim urgency but have no significant lasting consequence.

Professionals in student affairs are constantly confronting superficial fads and fashions that masquerade as precursors of far-reaching change. Because most leaders are wary about being regarded as slow to change or resistant to new ideas, there is often a propensity to regard new ideas and developments as inherently significant, especially if promulgated by individuals or organizations that have established reputations and credibility. No doubt many senior student affairs leaders have had my experience of working for an enthusiastic president who seems to want to reorganize the university every time he or she encounters a popular new management theory or organizational strategy.

A professional leader must learn to discern the change issues that will have enduring influence from those that are transitory. Enduring changes modify the status quo over time and create truly new conditions and circumstances. Some examples of enduring changes for student affairs work over the past two decades include student interest in apartment living, the community service movement, increasing diversity in higher education, the first-year experience, student involvement in recreation and fitness, profit-oriented enterprise activities in higher education, and increased careerism among college students. These trends changed our basic approaches to working with college students and altered our understanding about how to best serve their needs in these areas. Like most enduring changes, however, the trends emerged over time and could be detected by a close observation and monitoring of students' interests and needs.

The Nature of Change in Student Affairs Leadership

It is difficult to categorize all the changes that one is likely to confront in professional work in student affairs because of the unpredictable nature of both the profession and the process of change itself. However, the following eleven changes are some of the most important and challenging ones:

- Appointment of a new president
- Institutional or divisional reorganization
- Major new institutionwide initiatives
- New laws, regulations, policies from external sources; for example, legislature, boards of trustees, federal and state government
- Unanticipated economic changes; for example, loss or decline of resources, revenues, enrollment
- Change of jobs and institutions
- Catastrophic events; for example, fire, flood, student deaths, scandals
- Emerging trends in students' college preferences, career interests, and personal values
- New technology and technology infusion
- Key personnel changes
- Personal factors; for example, retirement, health, aging, burnout, family issues

In the following sections, our authors comment on some of these important change issues and the critical values issues they raise, the strategies they used to deal with such changes, and their personal observations about how the changes affected their professional work and personal lives.

Reorganization

One of the most time-consuming and disruptive aspects of professional practice is dealing with what sometimes appear to be perpetual reorganization and power shifts in university administration. Colleges and universities are, it seems, almost always engaged in the process of downsizing, right-sizing, expanding, reengineering, retrenching, or pursuing some bold new initiative. These changes may be initiated by factors external to the institution or they may simply be the result of internal power shifts in which new leaders emerge who bring new agendas of priority and change. The arrival of a new president on campus often is an occasion for reassessing institutional priorities and reorganizing staffing structures and administrative processes.

Organizational restructuring can be one of the most threatening changes that confront student affairs leaders. It can be threatening because it often involves the transfer of power and resources, as well as shifts in jobs and status. Student affairs leaders may feel the threat of reorganization more keenly than other institutional leaders because student affairs organizations typically have less status and power than other areas of college and university administration. Although most student affairs leaders want to be good team players and support efforts to improve institutional effectiveness, they are usually very conscious that they may have more to lose in the process than others.

As I (J.C.D.) reflect upon my own experiences of reorganization in several different universities, I must confess that I approached every one of them with some sense of dread and apprehension. One has the feeling that, from the standpoint of the student affairs organization, there is much to lose and not much to gain in such exercises. Depending on how aggressively and urgently the reorganization is driven, responses can be anything from collegial discussions to circling of the war wagons. Student affairs leaders who have endured several of these institutional upheavals often feel that they come along much too frequently and are enormously taxing on the energy and resources of leaders and staff. The irony is that in the end, the actual changes that result from most reorganization efforts seldom seem to merit all the commotion.

Managing the changes brought by reorganization initiatives does pose major challenges for student affairs leaders and must be well managed. These challenges require loyalty, effective teamwork, a willingness to think in new and different ways, and the skills to engage in high-stakes decisions and win-win situations in the sense of emerging from the process with sufficient resources and power to accomplish the student affairs mission. The pressure that this process places upon the student affairs leader can be especially taxing on the spirit.

Martha Sullivan reflects upon her experiences with reorganization and how she maintains a sense of balance and good humor in the midst of so much change:

Human nature does not always reveal its best side in times of stress. . . . The jostling for power during a rapid and seemingly endless series of reorganizations, restructurings, reengineering at my institution is an example that left us all reeling and bruised at every turn. When I found myself losing my sense of balance and certainly my sense of humor, I found great comfort, solace, and immeasurable wisdom in returning to the classics of my original field of study. The vain, self-important sycophants of the influential and powerful, the conniving, and the cunning depicted by the moralists in seventeenth-century France all have their easily identified counterparts on the modern American campus, particularly during times of major power shifts. Keeping La Bruyere and La Rochefoucauld by my bedside helped me immeasurably to put all the turmoil around me into perspective. At times I know my staff thought I had possibly gone off the deep end (or at least was being somewhat the stuffy intellectual) when I referred to these writers. But then again, maybe in some small way it reinforced for them the immense and usually intangible value of the liberal arts.

I keep on my computer a quote I like from Andy Grove when he was CEO of Intel Corporation: "Let chaos reign, then rein in chaos. Does that mean that you shouldn't plan? Not at all. You need to plan the way a fire department plans. It cannot anticipate fires, so it has to shape a flexible organization that is capable of responding to unpredictable events." I had never thought of us as being firefighters, but in many ways it does quite adequately describe . . . our role as campus crisis managers.

Martha found a way to keep a balanced perspective on the upheaval caused by reorganization by maintaining an intellectual and personal grounding in her academic discipline. Different student affairs leaders no doubt discover uniquely personal ways to maintain balance and perspective in tough times when the landscape is shaky and changing. Institutional reorganization is a type of change that requires student affairs leaders to be at their best so as to use their practical wisdom and leadership skills. It may well be one of their most defining roles.

Changes in Personnel

I (J.C.D.) remember a piece of advice offered to me early in my career. I am not sure who said it or what the occasion was, but I have long remembered the advice and have confirmed it over and over again in my experience. The advice was this: *Never underestimate a personnel problem!* One of the most important and unpredictable types of change that student affairs leaders must deal with is turnover or removal of personnel. The loss of key staff members can pose significant problems in a number of ways. The loss can put an operation at jeopardy with far-reaching consequences for students, staff, the student affairs organization, and the student affairs leader. I remember one occasion in which I had to personally take over the direct administration of one of the departments I supervised because of the incompetence of the director. I thought I could put things quickly in good order but I learned that there are more ways to get in trouble than I had ever dreamed!

Staff changes occur for many random and unpredictable reasons, such as professional moves, health problems, retirement, emergencies, special assignments, and failure to perform satisfactorily. Elizabeth Nuss discusses some situations she encountered with personnel issues and what she learned from these experiences:

> The new semester has started and once again there are some unanticipated staff issues. The director of residence life has accepted a new position and will be leaving at the end of January. It leaves a big hole in the division. While we had talked on earlier occasions about her desire to look at new opportunities and I was supportive of her personal needs, I naturally hoped it would occur at a different time. Not sure why I think a different time would be better. There is never a good time.
>
> The unit has many new and young staff and there is no clear person ready to take on duties even in the interim. I am weighing options of asking the associate dean or one of the other directors to take on some additional responsibilities. I'm feeling the pressures of the need to have conversations with several staff members to explore options and get their suggestions and ideas. The desire to be consultative, thoughtful, and deliberate weighs against the need to decide, move the process along, launch the search, hurry up, and identify someone. I am second-guessing myself and asking myself why I hadn't had these conversations before now. I knew she would eventually leave. But how could I have the conversations in the abstract? It would not have been ethical to talk with others about her plans.

Change in Jobs

One of the most important changes that all student affairs professionals must address at some time in their careers is when (or if) to make a significant job change. Deciding when to move and when to stay in one's current professional position can be a very stressful calculation. As we shall see in the reflections of our authors in this issue, advice differs on whether changing institutions is good for one's career development. Much depends upon the individuals and the circumstances of their work and personal life. But there is no disagreement that decisions about career changes almost always provoke serious introspection and reflection, and the decisions made in those situations often shape one's career for a lifetime. For me (J. C. D.) personally, decisions about career changes have been among the most difficult dilemmas of my professional work. Here are some thoughts from my journal:

Making job changes has been one of the most invigorating and yet agonizing aspects of my professional development. Experiences of beginning new jobs in different settings with new colleagues have been very energizing and positive for me. Every fresh start has been an opportunity to do things better, leave behind past mistakes, explore new territory. I learned I was capable of incredible concentration and workloads during transition periods and that I was highly motivated by new challenges and new experiences. Changing jobs has been for me a powerful stimulus for professional growth and learning.

I described the invigorating part; the agonizing part was just as intense. Every "hello" was also a "goodbye." New responsibilities meant leaving behind unfinished work. Change was hard on my family and weighed heavily on me. In a time of increasing cultural change and rootlessness, I worried about continually tearing up my own roots. I sometimes wondered if changing jobs reflected a lack of professional depth and commitment on my part. While I value change, my professional heroes and heroines have always been those who have worked long and successfully in one institution. Here there is no masking of talent and character.

Whether any professional move is "right" is a profoundly personal decision that depends on a lot of factors. In the end, for me at least, the desire to occasionally explore new places and roles always outweighed the negatives. I tried to change institutions about every eight or nine years, depending on family circumstances and opportunities. Changing jobs within an institution can also provide some of the same benefits of moving to another institution. I have held eight different student affairs jobs in four universities.

Many of the most successful student affairs leaders have opted to remain with one institution for a very long time. The advantages of longtime tenure in one institution are many, including opportunities to establish long-term friendships, stability for family and personal lifestyle, and the rewards of loyalty and long-term relationships.

Bud (William) Thomas retired as vice chancellor for student affairs at the University of Maryland–College Park after twenty-five years in the senior leadership role. In his reflections that follow, Bud looks back over his long service at the University of Maryland and comments on his convictions about working in one institution for many years, some of the strategies and approaches he used to achieve long-term effectiveness, and how he views the essential roles in student affairs leadership:

I remained at the University of Maryland for a long time because the presidents and chancellors had integrity. They did not go into scape-goating, and that can happen. It happened to a lot of my colleagues around the country. If you don't have a president that backs you, you're dead. You have to work at making presidents willing to back you, but they don't *have* to do that and they can remove you if the pressure builds sufficiently; it never happened to me and I'm lucky as hell. That's a quick answer.

Now how do you get that confidence? When I first came here, I concluded that athletics at Maryland was a big deal. I joined the Terrapin Club. I've been a member ever since I came here. Did that get me any leeway along the way? It probably did. I had to deal with athletic directors and coaches, but I was not known as an anti-athlete person. I understood the role of athletics at Maryland, at least well enough to know that it was going to outlast me. And I recognized that it had a significant role in the identification of students with the institution, as well as alumni and many other in the community. That was never going to go away. One has to recognize that. You have to make athletics the best it can be. I got a seat on the Athletic Council right after I got here. At one point I had to make a case to keep it. After that case, I've kept it, and I've kept it all that time. I was never without some knowledge of what they were doing, or without the opportunity to be supportive when I could be. That probably kept me from being at times an apparent enemy to athletics.

I happen to also have a few habits like golf and poker that put me in the company of some significant other people. Networking on a college campus is essential. Who you know might save your ass. I was conversant with some significant people in the community very early in my career in both social and business relationships, and these served me well. It also helps if you make an effort to understand the issues that you are dealing with and try to frame them with your boss and other colleagues in a way that will put a favorable light on the work of your people. If you are not in a room where an issue is being discussed, you can't usually influence the framing of that issue, so I went to meetings that other people may not have gone to and that helped.

The bottom line is about staying or going. If the president wanted me to go at any time, I would have gone. I always figured that if asked to leave I would negotiate and get a year so I could relocate. Even if I were asked to leave in three weeks I would try to negotiate for a year's salary, because I have family commitments. I think that's a reasonable thing for a vice president to negotiate.

On Dealing with Supervisors

Larry Roper reflects on one of the most important change issues in being a professional: how to develop and maintain a positive relationship with supervisors, especially when a new supervisor may set unrealistic or conflicting expectations. Finding your own appropriate balance and rhythm for work and personal life can be especially difficult if one's supervisor has conflicting values and expectations.

I have found one of the most difficult parts of developing balance in my work and life is managing the real and perceived demands of supervisors. At various times during my career I have found myself working with supervisors whose approaches to work did not model health and balance. I have had supervisors who arrived early and worked extremely late into the night as their normal routine. I have noticed that e-mail messages would be sent well after midnight on weeknights and weekdays. The imbalance they would show was manifested in not integrating exercise into their lives, not making time for relaxing meals, or not building vacations into their schedules. These unhealthy supervisors would flaunt their work schedules as a badge of honor in an effort to communicate their commitment to the organization. None ever said to me that they expected me to emulate their work behaviors.

Nonetheless, it was difficult to observe these behaviors and not take away an implicit message about what was expected of me regarding work style. As a young professional I attempted to emulate the unhealthy work styles, believing that such an approach modeled how to achieve success. As I gained more experience and developed more confidence and certainty about my aspirations, I became more capable of independently constructing a balanced work life. At the same time, it is an easy temptation to model your professional behaviors after the person who controls your livelihood.

I am constantly challenged to set limits on how much of myself I will give to my job. The difficulty arises in determining how to set limits while still communicating my desire to achieve excellence in my performance. It is important to set limits with unhealthy supervisors, especially those who believe that everyone should mirror their approach to work. For me it has been as simple as telling the supervisor I appreciate the commitment that he or she is capable of making; however, because of the commitments that I have in my life I will need to balance my life and achieve excellence in my work responsibilities in a different way. It is important to not demean or judge, but to clearly communicate that you are committed, but in a different way.

Not all supervisors will be gracious as you assert your desire to have a balanced life. However, I have found that most will respect your desire for a full life. It is the rare supervisor who is not capable of distinguishing between the number of hours you work and the quality of work that you produce.

On Matching Your Strengths to Your Institution's Needs

Most of us can no doubt deal with change and be successful professionals if we are fortunate to find the right "fit" between our talents and the particular needs of an institution. We are inclined at times to think that such "fit" is the luck of the draw, of being at the right place at the right time. Certainly chance plays a part in our own personal destinies, but as Margaret Barr describes in her reflection, we must have a high degree of self-awareness about our skills and abilities and make wise career choices that build on those strengths.

I don't know that I have gained wisdom about anything but I do know that I have learned a great deal about self and others during my thirty-five years in higher education. Part of that learning has come from working at five different institutions with five unique characters and sets of folkways and mores. I have learned that although institutions look remarkably the same they are remarkably different. I have learned that as the "new kid on the block" you need to be political in the best sense of the word and understand the history and tradition behind the often irrational organizational structures you encounter and policies that do not make sense on the surface. You also need to make sure that you understand your mandate and what others expect you to do.

On Being a Successful Change Agent

I suspect most student affairs leaders enjoy the process of change as long as they are the ones directing the enterprise and it helps to achieve the goals and priorities important to them. Facilitating changes that move organizations toward more effective operations and achievements is expected of most leaders, and they usually expect to have such roles. Effective leaders must be able to relish the tasks of change and lead the process with clarity of vision and personal energy. Sooner or later in the work of student affairs leadership, being a successful change agent is an essential role. It requires some special knowledge and skills in human psychology and behavior, research, strategic planning, communication, and political collaboration. It is an area of leadership that is challenging for the seasoned professional and often overwhelming for the inexperienced leader. Linda Reisser discusses some of the important tools she uses in managing change and provides a model for the change process that she has found useful in her change initiatives:

I have tended to see myself as a change agent, regardless of the setting I was in. This may be because wherever I have worked, I was on the lookout for discrepancies between how things were done and how they could be done better, in my humble opinion! I am also drawn to conferences and new approaches to theory and research. I'm sure my staff cringes when I return, armed with more ideas about reforming higher education. I have had to constantly remind myself that others are less comfortable with restructuring operations than I am, especially if I am initiating them.

I think I have become more effective at three tools for leading a change process:

Get the data. Displaying facts and findings in clear reports, bar graphs, and simplified findings makes a more powerful statement about what needs to be fixed. For example, an initiative to increase funding for student services was greatly helped by data showing our share of the budget declining, right along with the retention rate, even though enrollment was increasing.

Propose and implement a pilot project. Work with a "think tank" of committed change agents to develop a written proposal for a manageable project. Then carry it out and evaluate it. The organization is much more likely to adopt it if they can see what it looks like.

Manage the process. I have found that if I am initiating a change project, I usually need to take on the responsibility of planning the meetings, writing up the results, asking people to do specific things, negotiating with others to help, and so forth. I have not had as much luck turning a great idea over to a committee, unless the chair is as obsessive as I am.

Other key lessons I have learned regarding managing change:

Engaging support from the highest-level leaders is critical.

A strategic plan or set of mobilizing goals from the president or board may be helpful to create a readiness for change. But nothing will happen without an active and creative leader managing the change process.

Resources may or may not be critical; attitude is.

It's important to report on successes and celebrate them publicly.

Conclusion

Managing change is one of the central tasks of student affairs leadership and one of the areas of being a professional where practical wisdom is critical. Over the long haul of a career the ability to plan for and respond with creativity and flexibility to transforming changes is essential for success as a student affairs professional. Some changes are likely to be transforming and strategic for the student affairs professionals; some changes, if not most, will be more sound than substance. Knowing the difference is the art of practical wisdom. Entertaining new possibilities with flexibility and openness while honoring those things that are worthy and enduring and that provide continuity and meaning to people and organizations is one of leadership's greatest challenges.

Reference

Spencer, J. *Who Moved My Cheese?* New York: Putnam, 1998.

JON C. DALTON is associate professor of higher education and director of the Center for the Study of Values in College Student Development at Florida State University.

DIANA IMANUEL GARDNER is a second-year higher education master's student at Florida State University in the department of educational leadership.

The author discusses how senior student affairs administrators juggle busy lives and shares their recipes for maintaining healthy and balanced lifestyles.

5

Self-Renewal and Personal Development in Professional Life

Linda Reisser

I used to quip to my friends who were out running, lifting weights, and walking in the park that I was too tired to do any of that. Most of my weeks are mental marathons. When I came home at night, my only exercise was to fall asleep in my easy chair, in front of the TV. That's a portrait of someone whose life is not in balance. Our world presents us with more challenges, opportunities, and demands than we can handle, even with our emerging skill at multitasking. E-mail can speed communication and save paper but puts 150 messages a day on my electronic desk. We maintain our calm exterior (we hope) while holding stress about budget problems, discipline cases, staff concerns, and enrollment pressures. Students present a wider array of needs and issues every year, while our institutions skimp on the human infrastructure needed to support them. Yet as helping professionals we feel responsible for meeting the needs of those students, those of the frayed staff, and those of the organization itself. We also struggle with big projects that need our leadership, and as we know, those projects tend to be assigned to the truly dedicated and competent, heightening the threat of burnout. If we also bring our energy to the surrounding community, there may be precious little left for our own renewal. That's why it has become more important to consciously design ways to stay in balance and to renew mind, body, and heart.

Others have recognized this need. Art Sandeen writes:

> What keeps us going? Why do we need to renew ourselves? How do we keep learning? How do we avoid getting burned out? How do we live apart from our jobs? These are questions student affairs administrators ask themselves, and in

this regard we are no different from professionals in other fields. The pace of life gets faster every year; the demands of institutions increase, and our expectations for our own performance grow higher all the time. How, in the hectic, politically volatile world of student affairs administration do we make some sense of it all and at the same time renew ourselves and continue to grow?

Jon Dalton writes: "Certainly one of the most important challenges of professional success and fulfillment is how to continually renew one's energies and commitment. Burnout and boredom are not so much the consequences of doing the same things over and over again as they are the failure to periodically recharge one's spirit and enthusiasms. To be sure there is considerable repetition of tasks in professional work and prolonged periods of intensive efforts and stress, so it is essential to learn how to regenerate energies for sustained commitment."

It would be easy to pour all my energy into the projects determined by the college, even when most of the systems are working well. When crises occur or administrative tasks pile up in the funnel, our leadership responsibilities compete with our need for reflection time, inner work, and projects that we deem significant. We are still reeling from the tragedy of the World Trade Center attack and ensuing events on campuses and throughout the nation. That tragedy is a large-scale version of other challenges. We may feel wiped out after a week of hate speech issues, ecoterrorist attacks, student protests, unexpected budget cuts, breakdowns in equipment or facilities, disruptive changes in leadership, or demoralizing decisions. On a smaller scale, energy drainers include ongoing annoyances such as personnel problems, interpersonal conflicts, bureaucratic inefficiencies, or time-consuming conduct cases.

Each of us has to find ways to re-source ourselves. The cookbook of personal renewal has many recipes, and we need to taste many and choose the ones that nurture us most. As Art Sandeen says: "After having worked for thirty-eight years in administrative positions, I am now a professor, and this has enabled me to look back more objectively on my career—how I survived, how I found enjoyment, why I stayed so long, and how I tried to continue to learn. However, I would never suggest that my approach to these issues is something others should follow; to the contrary, these questions are very personal in nature, and others have to work them out in a way that makes sense to them."

Self-renewal and personal development are essential for all of us if we are to continue to grow and enjoy our lives. But we are all different, and what might work for one person has little relevance for another. The important thing is to discover what works for each of us and act upon it!

Renewal at Work

There are renewal experiences every day at the office, especially if we consciously co-create them. My most important ones involve savoring the relationships with students and staff. Collaborative work, flavored with laughter and personal sharing, adds enjoyment to a hectic week. I value time for meaningful dialogue, praise, and acknowledgement and stepping out of the trees to find meaning in the forest. I strongly believe in trying to be intentional about fostering an atmosphere of informality and enjoyment, with retreats, potlucks, humor, celebrations, and community-building traditions, such as holiday parties, retirement roasts, and sing-along parodies. I resonate with my colleagues who savor the new projects and kick-offs that start the fall term.

Art Sandeen writes:

> Like other senior student affairs officers, I had opportunities to do other things, but I knew what I liked to do and in particular I knew what I did not like to do in higher education. Thanks to the challenging presidents I worked for and the excellent student affairs colleagues I had, I could not imagine another job that would be any better, so I stayed. Before each new academic year began, I identified two or three new projects or ideas I would pursue. Some of these were with our staff or some other administrative area of the campus, and others were more personal in nature. Doing this enabled me to learn new things, try new ideas, and take some risks; all of these activities, of course, were related to continuing learning and self-renewal. I was well aware that it was a way to force myself to take on a new project or learn something new; at the end of the academic year, I didn't want to feel that I had done nothing but keep the plant running and put out fires.

Jon Dalton identifies a renewal source in projects that have personal significance:

> There are a few things that I have learned about self-renewal that have enabled me to sustain my love for my profession and my life beyond work. First, I have found that focusing on some special interests in my work provides a sense of accomplishment and personal growth over time. For me these interests have centered on the moral learning and development of college students. Serving as a senior student affairs leader for many years has forced me to learn much about a great many issues, but I have always managed to keep some special focus on moral and ethical issues in college student development. As I deepened my knowledge and expertise over time I found greater motivation to learn more and to seek the collaboration of others with similar interests. So I learned that plowing deep furrows brings its own good rewards and satisfactions. Having serious intellectual interests can sustain and renew one over a lifetime.

Others emphasize the rewards of working with students. Art Sandeen writes: "As I assess my administrative career, I am glad I made the effort to spend a lot of time with individual students; it gave me great joy, and now I wish I had done even more of it! While I am also glad I spent considerable time reading and writing, I know that my emotions and feelings drove my work more than my intellect or mind. Student affairs work is not very cerebral; it is mainly about passion!"

Renewal from External Activities

Sources for renewal abound outside our institutions. Colleagues echo one another in pointing to continuous learning, service activities, health and recreation, travel, cultural events, and the relational world of family, friends, and community involvement. These passions and diversions provide a needed break and new lenses. Art Sandeen writes:

> I was very fortunate to work with colleagues and presidents who were very stimulating and supportive. This made my work interesting, but every year I was greatly relieved when the academic year ended, as I was physically and emotionally tired due to the constant pressure and long hours. I found my self-renewal in family camping and fishing trips, in reading and writing, in playing squash, and in music. I could become so engaged in these activities that I could completely forget about my job. Most of all, I was fortunate to be married to a very independent woman who had her own career and personal interests and who regularly reminded me not to take myself so seriously.

Doris Ching writes of the importance of community work:

> One of the greatest joys I have experienced in my professional life is the privilege of giving. Community service and contributing have been a way of life for me since I was in the first grade. I was thrilled to spend my recess periods packing personal care boxes for the American Red Cross and took great joy assuring that the toothbrush, comb, pencil, note pad, and other essential items were neatly arranged so that they fit in the container. I recall how I looked forward to wearing my red feather each year when I gave my dime to the Community Chest, the forerunner of the United Way. Still, the discovery of just how rewarding giving to charity and professional causes can be has far surpassed my expectations. Such contributions have literally become contributions to myself.

She also sees rewards in giving to the profession:

> Giving is a way to give back to a fulfilling profession that has given me countless opportunities to grow. Giving is to know that I have a part in strengthening the future of the profession and believing I can help to make a difference in this world.
>
> Another discovery I made early in my administrative career, as a new associate dean of education, is that higher executives in colleges and universities equate giving with commitment. Voluntary donations to various causes

in my institution were consistent with my giving philosophy. I did not anticipate the notice that would be given to the contributions by the higher ups,
who were already recognizing my effectiveness as an administrator. Thus,
while my performance was certainly not measured by the donations, I believe
the recognition was enhanced at this early stage of my career by the giving.

Charles Schroeder underscores the value of continuous learning and
the juggling of priorities to find balance:

During the past thirty-five years, I have served in a variety of administrative
roles in student affairs, including being a chief student affairs officer (CSAO)
in four institutions since 1998. Like most CSAOs, my professional life was
incredibly demanding and intense—my days usually started at 5 A.M. and
would occasionally end at 10 P.M. with the conclusion of an evening commitment at the university. Because of my professional activities, the intensity
spilled over into most weekends, when I usually worked two to three hours
on Saturday and Sunday mornings developing presentations, writing manu-
scripts, or simply trying to stay ahead of the game. The challenge for me, as
well as for many of my CSAO colleagues, was to "find balance" in my life.

A few years ago my friend and colleague Jim Hurst delivered the keynote
address at the Missouri College Personnel Association. In his address, Jim
talked about the need for balance in one's life, and he shared a very vivid
experience he had as a child. He recalled going to a county fair, where he
observed four acrobats who whirled around the arena while suspended from
a fifty-foot pole. Suddenly, one of the acrobats lost his balance and all four
fell to their death. I've thought about this story often as I have reflected on
our profession's commitment to the "holistic" development of our students—
focusing on the intellectual, affective, spiritual, and physical dimensions of
self. Certainly, in an ideal world, we as professionals would try to find balance in our lives by devoting appropriate time and energy to each of the
domains. In reality, however, we are often like the acrobats who perished
because of the imbalance in the system. So what can we do about it?

For me, personal renewal is much more of a continuous process than an
episodic event. Physical fitness, for example, has always been a critical focus
of my life and I work hard at ensuring that fitness is a constant personal priority. Hence, I work out a minimum of five times a week and rarely let other
things interfere with this commitment. In retrospect, I wish I had devoted as
much discipline and tenacity to my spiritual development, which, in many
cases, has provided much deeper fulfillment than physical activity. In addition to devoting time to fitness and spiritual issues, I find tremendous enjoyment and fulfillment in my family relationships and periodic sojourns in the
mountains.

As important as my work and professional commitments have been, I
have always placed family first. In this regard, I never missed any of my son's
high school football, basketball, or baseball games and I always attended all
of my daughter's social and athletic events. Similarly, I have always been

renewed by a variety of adventure-oriented activities—downhill skiing, rock climbing, skydiving, hunting, backpacking, and various trips throughout the world. Having recently transitioned from a chief student affairs role to a teaching role, I realize now, more than ever, that life is not a dress rehearsal. This is it! Hence, I am devoting more and more of my discretionary time to a series of daily and weekly activities that provide deeper meaning for my life, praying, daily workouts, quiet time with my wife, and plans for more time in the mountains.

Renewal from Inner Work

Balancing and focusing are acts of will that are needed to restore the different rooms in our house of self. For my students, I often diagrammed Sharon Wegscheider's (1981) model of the personality in the form of a wheel with six segments: physical, mental, emotional, social, spiritual, and volitional. The volitional part of self is the ability to focus, prioritize, and persist toward important goals. She felt that all segments needed to be strong and in balance or the wheel would begin to wobble, especially in a crisis.

Larry Roper reflects this holistic approach to finding inner balance:

> Throughout my career one of my most significant struggles has been to maintain balance in my life. I have found that it is easiest to maintain balance when there is something in my life that I have determined to be more important than my job and when I actively work to live as if that aspect of my life is most important. At the same time, whenever I find myself feeling or thinking that my job is the most important aspect of my life or identity, I invariably end up feeling out of balance.

Balance

Balance to me is that sense of wholeness that I get from the recognition that the foundation of my life, identity, and existence rests upon something that is life-sustaining potential and that can be a source of wellness for me. No matter how generous I have tried to be toward the many wonderful and fulfilling jobs I have held, none of them could be described as possessing life-sustaining potential. The conditional nature of support in most work settings, the instability that characterizes many institutions, and the general lack of recognition for the total humanity of workers have led me to believe that a job is not the axis upon which I wish to have my life revolve. A job can be the source of wonderful relationships, accomplishments, enrichment, joy, and many other positive experiences. But this should not be mistaken for life.

At various points in my career I have shifted the balance of my life among a number of different essential ingredients: healthy mind, healthy body, healthy relationships, healthy spirit, healthy community, and a healthy sense of humor. Throughout life the centerpiece of the balance I seek has shifted as I have struggled with different aspects of my personal growth. However, most consistently, having a healthy spirit has been the major focus of my life. To me, a healthy spirit is being in touch with a sacred energy source. When I am spiritually healthy my sacred source gives me energy for living and sustains me during trying times. I attend to my spiritual health through prayer, reflection, and renewal.

Perspective, Fitness, Family, Friends

Having a healthy mind means attempting to keep life and the events that occur in a proper perspective. I have struggled to maintain an outlook that does not cause me to distort either the positive or the negative that invariably takes place. Physical health is an important component of my ability to maintain a healthy and positive outlook on life. I have found that if a focus on fitness moves too far from the center of my life, the quality of my thinking and interactions with others also diminishes. Throughout my life my family has been the most consistent anchoring point for healthy relationships. At the same time, I have worked hard to stay aligned and engaged with a core group of close friends. My friends serve as sources of support, perspective, and challenge and are essential to my ability to stay grounded in reality. Most important, having a healthy family life where I am an active and meaningful contributor has emerged as the most powerful variable in my life and in defining my personal success. Nothing is more important than being a good father and husband.

Community

I can't recall a time in my life when being part of a healthy community has not been important to me. However, I have felt myself gradually mature and grow in my outlook on what my contribution should be to creating and sustaining a community. Contributing to community and acting in service to others plays a significant role in how I view having balance in my life. Part of balance, to me, is being in touch with and enhancing the shared humanity of those with whom I am in community.

Attitude—Humor

Finally, I attempt to maintain a healthy sense of humor. I try hard to take life and my work seriously but not to take myself too seriously. Laughter and humor provide a vehicle for maintaining a positive perspective.

I have found that when I am able to attend to the overall health of my life, I am able to maintain a more healthy approach to my profession. But during those times when I allow my professional responsibilities to take and hold center stage in my life, my professional performance diminishes.

Focusing on renewal activities involves letting go of other diversions. Time begins to look like it might run out when we get into our fifties. Choosing how to use it becomes more critical. Jon Dalton writes:

> I got good advice early. My seventh-grade teacher, Mrs. Adams, told me to concentrate on one thing and not to spread myself so thin. I was singing in the choir, playing football, working a paper route, trying to impress the new girl sitting next to me in class, and not doing so well in my schoolwork. Mrs. Adams thought I could accomplish more if I focused my efforts on a few things and did them well. As I recall, I decided to concentrate on the new girl.
>
> I had some similar advice from my freshman English professor in college who told me that I was capable of better work than I was doing. The fact that he cared enough to stop me after class with his advice still stays with me.
>
> It took me a while but I did take their good advice and over many years have managed to better focus my interests and energies. I learned the hard way what they say about an undisciplined and unfocused life. I learned to narrow and deepen my commitments and interests, and this has served me well over many years.
>
> I also learned that there is another kind of risk down the narrowing road of deep commitment. The risk is that there can be too much focus, too much concentration, especially when it comes to one's career. One of the serious risks of too much concentration on work-related tasks is long-term burnout. I traveled that road a few times.
>
> I did not, however, follow all of my mentors' advice! There are just too many interesting things in life to focus on only a few. There has to be a place for other passions and diversions in order to rekindle one's energies and motivations. For me these passions have included such things as running, sailing, traveling, and cooking . . . largely in this order of importance. In recent years I have found painting to be a wonderful means of expression and fulfillment. As with most of my passions, I have never found the lack of talent to be a significant barrier to personal fulfillment.
>
> What I have learned about personal renewal is that it helps greatly to cultivate interests in many things, to do things regularly that delight you and that rekindle a deep sense of joy and celebration. Many of the most successful student affairs professionals I know seem to exhibit strong creative outlets and deep personal interests.

It is an act of will to cultivate passionate interests, holistic balance, humor, and patience. I also need time by myself, without distractions, to reflect, rest, and see not only what is out of balance but also what is calling me to do for my own growth. I have become better at reminding myself that my worth and identity are not based on my professional roles. Like Art Sandeen, I am still working on patience and savoring solitude:

> Our work puts us in almost constant contact with people, and of course, most of us love this! Most student affairs administrators are gregarious by nature,

and we probably do our best work when mingling with others, talking, and arranging things! This was my favorite part of our profession, but I understood early in my career that I also needed my lonesome time every day. I found my solace by reading for an hour in bed each night—almost always something completely unrelated to student affairs. Without this quiet nightly ritual, and the wonderful things I read, I doubt that I could have survived the job.

Among the most important things I tried to learn was that I was not my job. I tried not to define myself or my life in terms of my job and tried to develop a strong sense of personal identity that was not dependent upon having any job. I loved my work, but I was convinced I would be the same person, regardless of the job I might have in life.

Finally, I surely would have been better at self-renewal and personal development if I had not been in such a hurry all the time or hadn't taken some campus problems so seriously. It bothered me too much when I couldn't settle problems or issues as fast as I thought I should. Moreover, when I encountered excessive bureaucracy or needless rules, I often was too impatient. Worst of all, I fooled myself into believing that being with my children on Sunday mornings might compensate for not seeing them much during the week.

I find myself focusing more on personal growth and the expansion of my own potential as a prescription for renewal. I need conferences, retreats, and workshops that invite me to take inventory of my own leading edges and commit to nurturing them. I am drawn not only to the usual national and regional conferences but also to smaller scale conferences that include interactive discussions, such as one in February 2001 at Pierce College in Washington state, called Head, Heart, and Hands. It focused on how to integrate objective learning with personal experience, often in a learning community. The presenters and participants not only shared deeply on a personal level but also read their poems, sang their songs, and participated in experiential exercises.

Traveling with people who are journeying as a learning experience renews me. I am renewed by plays, movies, and concerts that engage me intellectually and emotionally. I seek out teachers who help me see new realities; collaborators who invite me to write, produce, and generate creative projects; performers who inspire me with authenticity and originality. I thrive on lectures and workshops that help me reframe reality, such as a recent tour de force evening with Deepak Chopra, who brought the strange world of quantum physics into harmony with Eastern mysticism.

I have come to see my work as part of a larger Work that has to do with transformation of the self and society. This was heightened during a self-created sabbatical, when I left one job without another one to start. I found myself serendipitously at a lecture by Joseph Campbell. I had all kinds of epiphanies based on his ability to articulate a worldview that was entirely new to me—finding meaning by using symbols, archetypes, and metaphors. His book *The Hero with a Thousand Faces* (1990 [1949]) gave me the courage to continue into the wilderness, facing trials and revelations and returning to the community to add whatever revitalizing contribution I had brought back. I have sought out other writers and teachers who help move me out of the mundane, the tribal, the group psyche and into the individualizing, archetypal, and spiritual levels of understanding and meaning-making.

I look for teachers and collaborators who can help me expand awareness and productivity. Art Chickering gave me the gift of his theory and the chance to collaborate in extending it. Diane Pike helped me reframe life with principles from ancient wisdom. Jean Houston helped me tune into my own *entelechy*, a Greek term meaning "dynamic, directed, guided purpose." Jean Houston (personal communication, September 18, 2001) calls us to see our role in a large human drama and make a conscious choice about how to use our creativity to participate in the needed transformations:

> We are the ones who have the most profound task in human history . . . the task of deciding whether we grow or die. This will involve helping cultures and organizations move from dominance by one economic culture or group to circular investment, sharing, and partnership. It will involve putting economics back as a satellite to the soul of culture rather than having the soul of culture as satellite to economics. It will involve deep listening past the arias and the habits of cruelty of crushed and humiliated people. It will involve a stride of soul that will challenge the very canons of our human condition. It will require that we become evolutionary partners with each other.
>
> In these spirit quaking times, align with your own spiritual resources. Take time to meditate, pray, reflect in solitude and in nature. Allow yourself daily time and space to be re-sourced. Consider living daily life as spiritual exercise. Watch your finer intuitions and ideas, and share them with others. Commune with your spiritual allies, archetypal friends, and quantum partners. In the place of spiritual connection feel strength and compassion and intelligence flow. Become creative in your actions. Plot scenarios of optimal healing and begin wherever you can to put them in place for events as well as people. Practice miracle management.

Houston exhorts us to renew ourselves by moving beyond serial monotony. Like others, who founded the human potential movement and joined the causes of civil rights, women's rights, gay rights, multicultural and diversity initiatives, welfare reform, and other concerted efforts to remove the barriers to achieving full potential, we need to acknowledge that we are in the right place at the right time—the opportunity factory called higher education. There we can foster the development of all parts of the self—our own and our students'—and in so doing, we align with the deeper purposes related to healing lives and empowering creative potential.

David Roth (1998) incorporated teachings from life into a song. These were gleaned from statements (some of which were included in the book

Live and Learn, Pass It On by H. Jackson Brown, Jr.) from people aged five to ninety-five. Completing the sentence, *I have learned . . .*

> That if you're not living on the edge, you're probably taking up too much room
> That you shouldn't go through life with a catcher's mitt on both hands; you need to be able to throw something back
> That even when you have pains, you don't have to be one
> That like that sign in Las Vegas says, You must be present to win.
> ("I Have Learned" ©1998 David Roth/Maythelight Music (ASCAP). Lyrics reprinted with permission.)

We need consciousness work aimed at fostering our own competence, purpose, integrity, identity, and relationships. We need to keep learning and acknowledge and pass on what our most important learning has been. That helps others find renewal from our journeys. We can renew others and ourselves by living on the edge, giving back, being a balm rather than a pain, and being fully present to the individuals and events on our path.

References

Campbell, J. *The Hero with a Thousand Faces.* Princeton, NJ: Princeton University Press (1990 [1949]).

Houston, J. Personal communication, received on Sept. 18, 2001 at [http://www.jean-houston.org].

Roth, D. "I Have Learned." CD, *Irreconcilable Similarities.* Chicago: Wind River Records, 1988. [http://www.folkera.com/windriver/davidroth]

Wegscheider, S. *Another Chance.* Palo Alto, Calif.: Science and Behavior Books, 1981.

LINDA REISSER *is the dean of student development at Portland Community College, Cascade Campus. She coauthored* Education and Identity, *2nd edition, with Arthur Chickering (Jossey-Bass, 1993), and contributed to* Good Practice in Student Affairs: Principles to Foster Student Learning *(Jossey-Bass, 1999) and* Life at the Edge of the Wave: Lessons from the Community College *(NASPA Monograph Series, 1998).*

6

Student affairs leaders describe why ethical considerations are so critical for making tough decisions and resolving complex problems in everyday work.

The Moral Domain of Student Affairs Leadership

William Thomas

At its core, student affairs leadership centers around ethical values, integrity, and the courage to do the right thing at the right time. Leaders are not immune to occasional doubt about what is the right thing to do, but they are guided by core values. Leadership is about commitment. Effective leaders are almost always characterized by personal convictions about what is good and worthy. In the work of student affairs, commitment usually includes loyalty to our institution, our leaders, and followers; the learning, development, and welfare of students; and a recognizable set of guiding values and ethical principles. Purposeful leadership is most often honored, whereas unprincipled, uncommitted leadership is rarely honored or effective.

In this chapter our contributors share some particularly significant experiences that they remember most vividly from among thousands of day-to-day issues, decisions, conflicts, and encounters. These experiences are remembered, no doubt, because they were difficult. The contributors were tested by circumstances with potentially serious outcomes, and they were forced to act. This chapter captures some of the special moments in which leaders have either forged their own value commitments or learned the hard way that values and integrity cannot be ignored.

Linda Reisser writes:

> Integrity has been important to me throughout my career, and especially when I see the consequences of damaged credibility. I have tried to act in congruence with personal and professional values and have encouraged staff to do so, by disseminating documents such as ACPA's "Statement of Ethical

Principles and Standards." I have seen how difficult it is to regain full confidence and respect after a leader's actions are perceived as arbitrary, unfair, or unethical. Members of a college community tune in quickly to the leader's core values, and if they come to feel that he or she is fair, honest, competent, and genuinely caring about the interests of the whole organization, they offer respect and allegiance. Conversely, if they see the leader as partial to some people or programs over others, or prone to cave in to political pressures, or more adept in rhetoric than listening to the real needs of the students or staff, the undercurrents of resentment and distrust create organizational toxins.

One way that staff members gauge integrity is by observing how the leader deals with recurring performance problems. Most people know where the problems are, and if they are allowed to continue without corrective action, cynicism and resignation result. I have tried to muster the will to confront those problems, documenting the discrepancies between what needs to happen and what the worker is or is not doing by writing specific work plans and offering assistance to improve, monitoring closely, and initiating action if corrections are not made.

I've found it very important to monitor newly hired employees carefully, since it's easier to undo a hiring decision if the person is still a probationary employee. But most of the problems I've dealt with have been long-term employees whose patterns have been tolerated for years. Examples include employees who were chronically late or absent, discourteous to students, unwilling to maintain professional case files, indiscreet in sharing information, or resistant to learning new computer systems. Several retired or left, once they realized I was going to sustain the effort to monitor their compliance and confront instances of noncooperation. In one case, an employee was regularly asleep in his office. He denied that there was a problem until we documented it and set up formal meetings with the human resource staff and a union representative. It was a stressful process, but the final outcome was that he was diagnosed with sleep apnea, a potentially life-threatening condition.

For me the greatest ethical challenges have been (1) discomfort with the ethics of a supervisor's decision and (2) controversial decisions involving conflicts between principles. In both cases I have learned to seek lots of consultation and a team approach to finding solutions that cause the least amount of damage. Examples of the first type include high-level administrators or board members asking for special treatment for friends or relatives. Each time this has happened, I have been dumbfounded that they were insensitive to morale problems that ensue when it's obvious that we're interviewing someone's spouse or offspring because of their relationship instead of their credentials. I have also seen the image of the institution suffer when a student reporter got wind of this kind of nepotism and brought it to light through the media. I have been mentored by those more politically astute to say "Let me think about that before I respond," whenever my internal ethics-violation barometer starts to go through the roof, and then try to find a graceful way to resolve it without violating principles.

Examples of the second type include uproars over controversial speakers or events, and pressure from opponents. Sometimes the chief student affairs officer is the main articulator of a presenter's first amendment rights and the court precedents requiring colleges to allow free speech. I once defended a student organization's right to sponsor an erotic film festival, despite threats from alumni to cease donations and major skittishness by the president and public information office. A compromise was to institute a panel discussion prior to the films to inject some academic discourse into the event (while the impatient student audience blew up condoms and bounced them around like beach balls). However, I have instituted more protective procedures for renting space to off-campus groups, such as requiring insurance, charging the group for extra security, and reserving the right to review the agreement if we determine that it is a high-risk activity. This strategy led to cancellation of a video presentation by the Earth Liberation Front after some angry phone calls alerted us to their inflammatory poster. The lesson was one that I learned long ago in enforcing the conduct code that we need to have a good set of procedures and follow them closely, regardless of the nature of the incident.

In her reflections on leadership and values, Elizabeth Nuss shares a poignant experience of a situation involving a conflict in values.

This afternoon two students ask to see me about a friend. They talk with me about another student who left school early last fall as a result of serious mental health issues. They are very worried about her. They report that she stopped taking her medication and has been agitated more frequently and unable to sleep. They now believe she has a gun but they have not seen it. They report statements she has made about taking her own life. I explain that a faculty member expressed concern about her well-being last week and I am scheduled to meet with her tomorrow. I explain that under these circumstances I will need to talk with mental health professionals and campus safety. I realize that when students become this concerned it really makes me more nervous. They typically have a higher threshold or tolerance for this kind of talk and behavior.

The conversation with campus security leads to a consultation with a workplace violence expert on the county police force. After a few hours they call back to indicate that after checking and consultation they believe they must begin their standard operating procedure and indicate that they will go to her apartment.

After searching her car and apartment they find no weapon. The student is furious. Her parents—divorced—both call to express their anger over the way the situation was handled. How could we believe their child had a weapon? I wonder what newspapers they read? I process the events of the last forty-eight hours quite a bit. Did I overreact? What other steps would I or could I have taken? I am influenced by the news of school shootings, workplace violence, and domestic violence that permeates our news.

Jon Dalton is a committed spokesperson for the recognition of ethics and values as a primary framework of our professional work. He argues that a professional must "profess" core values and be guided by them.

Ethics is an inescapable part of being a professional. A professional is someone who not only practices a discipline or skill but who also works within the framework of guiding moral principles. A professional is someone who "professes" certain beliefs and values and seeks to live and work according to them. Every genuine profession has guiding values that form its public credo. For the profession of student affairs these values and beliefs are articulated in the ethics statements of the student affairs–related associations.

In addition to professional ethics, all people have values and beliefs that they bring with them to work that, together with professional ethics, form their core moral values. The best professionals, those who have risen to the first ranks of leadership and reputation, almost always profess and practice a strong core of values.

Values keep our work on track. They serve as guideposts for what matters most in our work. They help us make tough decisions and give continuity to our leadership and example. They help keep order in the wide array of choices that one must face and make it possible to sleep at night after agonizing over conflicts and dilemmas. They make it possible to take unpopular stands when taking the easy way is so inviting. They give one an enduring place to stand in the midst of constant change.

The core values I have prized most in my professional work are integrity, respect for others, and compassion. Integrity is honesty in action, faithfulness to one's word, and consistency in word and action. I think it is the bedrock value of effective student affairs leadership.

Respect for others makes possible positive human relationships. Practicing this value can cover a multitude of sins.

Compassion is a constant reminder that everyone fails and that leadership must be tempered with understanding. Compassion makes it possible to accept our own failures and mistakes as well as others'. Over the years I have found myself returning to these three core beliefs, and they have been the most important guideposts for my journey in the profession.

Martha Sullivan describes a difficult values conflict situation she confronted and the complex issues and challenges it posed for her.

When I was quite new in student affairs, one of our student groups wanted to bring Meir Kehane to campus to speak, and I was given the contract to sign. A great deal of violence seemed to follow Kehane and I was concerned. I was a firm believer in freedom of speech. At the same time, I was fearful for the safety of our students. I took my dilemma to our senate committee on student affairs to ask for advice. I explained that I kept thinking of what I would do with my own two children. I was certainly not afraid for them to hear the content of Kehane's speech, but out of concern for their physical safety I would probably not allow them to go to his talk. This provoked an excellent discussion between the faculty and students on the committee, one that many of them will probably remember for many years.

The students later decided to rescind their offer, for a multiplicity of reasons not all related to this particular issue. The president later related to me that he had waited without intervening while I went through this process, noting that he would have overruled me had I not signed, because he felt that the speech issue was too important not to uphold. What would I do now? I would probably still take it to the committee, hoping to provoke yet another healthy discussion, but would then make certain our security was excellent and issue the invitation.

When I once complained as a teenager that I had not done something that my father questioned me about, he reminded me that often we not only have to do the right thing but we also need to look like we are doing the right thing. I have found this phrase, this dictum, useful throughout the years: You not only have to do the right thing, you often also need to look like you are doing the right thing.

Values Guide Leaders

There are many values that guide us in the challenges of delivering a wide range of growth-producing educational experiences to students. From my experience some of the most important values in our work include integrity, personal achievement, the common good of the community, safety, tolerance, respect for law, self-discipline, self-fulfillment, work ethic, compassion, democracy, confidentiality, accountability, teamwork, and independence. We often experience these values to be in conflict in our work. Effective leaders learn how to work with values in tension and to resolve them in ways that achieve the greatest good.

Ethical leaders in American higher education earn that distinction because they are able to articulate and put into practice a core of ethical values. I have found that this is not so hard to do in given instances but very difficult to do consistently over time. Why is it so hard to be consistently ethical? I suspect it is because of relentless changes occurring in such areas as institutional priorities, societal expectations, the requirements of law, evidence of what works and doesn't, our bosses and subordinates. What works, what makes moral sense, in one instance can change in the next. Jon Dalton comments on the additional problem of differing levels of individual concern about values and the problem of inconsistent ethical practice: "It has been my experience that different individuals have differing levels of awareness and commitments to ethics in their professional life. Some take ethics very seriously whereas others give them hardly any attention. Many profess but do not practice. Almost all who profess sometimes fail."

In spite of these uncertainties, we have benefited from the ruts of wagons of those who have gone before us. The ruts weave about and wander at times, but over time and much usage they make a road to follow. The road is a well-worn way of personal and professional integrity that is defined by values tested over time and circumstances. Ethical leaders do their best to follow the tested road, and most do so more often than not.

It is my experience that much of our work must be about the building of a culture where values are respected and valued. An ethical culture is a collegiate environment that defines a way of life and makes possible a community of character. We establish democratic procedures and organizations in a social process that incorporates the values and rights of individuals. We create policies that embrace and teach values such as order, fairness, due process, timeliness, and productivity. We judge performances of individuals in hundreds of ways, every day, every interaction, based on values such as achievement, productivity, style, integrity, appearance, and associations. I think all that is good and proper. If we did otherwise as a society, if we did not knowingly engage in, enjoy, and promote a culture of values in which all participate, how would moral values be conveyed and practiced? How would some of our most precious values survive the self-serving exercises of power by those who have little conscience? Thus, we deal in sowing, nurturing, and growing values. Our success in this process is demonstrated in the strength and acceptance of commonly held values in our collegiate communities.

Clearly, the most potentially compromising ethical arena for the chief student affairs officer is dealing with those who possess authority and especially those who have the power to hold us accountable for our decisions and actions related to our areas of assignment. Doris Ching reflects on an experience related to an encounter with issues of power and accountability.

> Being professional sometimes means facing painful tasks and making tough decisions, all for doing what is right—for students, for the institution, and for fellow professionals. In one such case, I faced all of these and the risk of being ostracized by my president. The case involved the chancellor of a smaller campus in the university system who was hired by the president. Although it did not involve my campus in any way, I got pulled into the tense and sensitive situation.
>
> When the new chancellor arrived at the campus, the entire university was thrilled that the small campus could attract a chief executive officer with such lofty stature and impressive credentials. The thrill turned to concern when the chancellor sometimes retreated behind the closed doors of his office for days, refusing to schedule meetings and appointments. The concern turned to shock when the chancellor unilaterally and haphazardly cut budgets and reorganized units, with no apparent logic or reason. Concern, shock, and confusion turned to desperation when the chancellor hired a dean of students

who had no higher education experience, other than being president of the athletic boosters club. By this time, approximately two years had passed since the chancellor's arrival.

The student leaders and student affairs professionals of the campus came to me in despair. Could I help? Did I know of a resource at the national level to which they could refer? They needed assistance and did not know where to turn. Their campus looked as though Hurricane Iniki, the most disastrous hurricane in the history of the state, had gone through it. How painful to stand by and say I had no jurisdiction over their campus or their chancellor. Was there anything I could do?

The dilemma found its way to the ears of the chairs of the board of regents and the board's student affairs committee. The regents discussed the matter with the president. No action was taken, and the campus situation worsened.

A small miracle occurred. The chair of the board of regents asked me to arrange a meeting for him with students and student affairs staff of the campus. I informed the offices of the board of regents, the president, and the chancellor that I was asked to do this and, hearing no objection, asked the student leaders of the campus to arrange the meeting. Two regents, including the chair, and I entered the meeting room. To our surprise, the assembled group included the campus's most highly respected academic faculty, researchers, and administrative staff—all of whom openly and candidly told their "horror stories" of devastation caused by "the administration." After the meeting, I left the room drained of emotion, devastated, in wonderment that any student or professional could function in such an unproductive and unpredictable environment.

I had no further conversation on the matter with either regent following the meeting. Months later, I learned that the chancellor had resigned the position and accepted a position elsewhere. The most appropriate word to describe the chair of the board is discreet. Surely, the faculty and staff of the campus and I hold him in the highest regard for his important role in preventing more damage to the campus and in changing its climate.

I never questioned myself for responding to the request of the board chair, even when the president was disapproving. I have never regretted the risk I took in arranging the meeting. Although I continued the positive relationship with my president, I know he was unhappy and annoyed with my part in the action. I don't believe he ever fully forgave me for the outcome. Nonetheless, my conscience is clear. I took action discreetly but openly, informing all affected offices prior to doing so. Though it was a painful process, it was also cleansing and fulfilling in the sense of professional responsibility. The president did not deny my observation that he would have been in jeopardy as president had I not facilitated the chancellor's departure.

How will I know when a cherished value violated is more than I can bear? Often we have wrestled with that question. It is probably the bottom-line question in any discussion of ethics in our workplace.

Charles Schroeder has gone farther than many to live a life that is consistent with his personal values. He discusses his guiding values and the role they play in his educational philosophy:

> During my thirty-five-year tenure in student affairs, I have encountered a wide range of perspectives, attitudes, and beliefs about our profession. One perspective, however, has consistently disturbed and perplexed me. That is, the all too common self-flagellating, Rodney Dangerfield attitude, "we don't get no respect." This all too common attitude has bothered me for decades and yet I have found solace in Elizabeth Blake's assertion that "the best solution is not to claim professional standing but to show it." So what does it mean to be a true student affairs professional? Undoubtedly, answers to this question will reflect differences in personal values, administrative styles and orientations, institutional settings, and personality styles and preferences. For me, however, the most important response is simply this—tie what you do to what matters most in your institution. Our work is, first and foremost, educational by nature; therefore, we are obligated and bound to enhance the quality of undergraduate education at our institutions by working cooperatively with our academic colleagues to enhance student learning and student success. In my experience, this has required me to be a very vocal and visible advocate for undergraduate education reform: for extending the conversation beyond the often narrow emphasis on the core curriculum to include the importance of core experiences; from exclusively teaching-centered and staff-centered environments to student learning–centered environments; from what is customarily academic to what is uniquely educational. Extending the conversation requires a vision of education and a willingness to make more permeable the tightly bound borders that separate academic affairs and student affairs. It also requires challenging fundamental assumptions about the nature of our work and asking ourselves *why* we are doing this as well as *how* we can do it better.
>
> In reflecting on my own journey to become an effective professional, nothing has affected me more than my participation in 1995 in a twenty-three-day Outward Bound course in the Sawtooth Primitive Area of Idaho. Among other things, the course taught me the significant role that core values, high expectations, and tenacity play in fostering personal and professional success. It also taught me lifelong lessons about people—that is, people are much more capable than they think they are and the role of education is to actualize that potential. Hence, for me, being an effective professional requires high expectations of self and others, an obligation—even a duty, if you will—to stay current in the field and to be true to one's personal values. With regard to values, I carry in my wallet, at all times, a small laminated red card that was given to me by a lieutenant colonel in the U.S. Marine Corps. The card is carried by all active duty Marines and includes the three core values of the Corps: *honor* (integrity, responsibility, accountability),

courage (do the right thing, in the right way, for the right reasons), and *commitment* (devotion to the Corps and to my fellow Marines). Obviously, these are espoused values of the Marine Corps and the real test, for Marines and others, is to make sure there is a tight coupling between espoused values and values in practice. For me, that is the essence of being a professional— being clear, consistent, and transparent with regard to personal and professional values; acting on your values even when the action might jeopardize your position at the institution.

So for me, being a professional means tying what I do to what really matters to my institution, having high expectations for self and others, acting with integrity, being tenacious and persevering in the face of adversity, and being willing to take reasonable risks.

Larry Roper discusses the special responsibility student affairs professionals have when they accept authority for managing complex organizations:

Sociologist W.E.B. DuBois described the challenge of the African American experience by saying, "nobody can live in the middle all of the time." This phrase can easily be used to describe the challenge of being a senior student affairs officer. I have found leading a student affairs organization to be a challenging and opportunity-rich role. The role requires that I be on everybody's side, which allows me to be a potential ally to everyone. But the role also challenges me because during times of challenge and conflict others expect me to choose sides. As the leader of an organization charged with responsibility for representing and supporting the growth of all students, it has been important that I learn to manage challenges to and conflicts in values. The place where the difficulty of being in the middle has most often surfaced for me has been the management of diversity conflicts. Specifically, in the face of a racial, anti-Semitic, or homophobic incident, I have been challenged to make real the responsibility of being on everybody 's side. In the face of such incidents I have been called upon to make assertive statements and exhibit definitive actions to illustrate my and the institution's commitment to diversity. At the same time, I have been required by my role to sit in judgment of the behavior. The difficulty of such situations is balancing my own personal reactions to a hateful activity with my responsibility to care for the community and my responsibility to respond to an issue in a way that says I care for the offending student. As the person most in the middle I need to be the one to bring the greatest amount of balance to how the issue is viewed and responded to.

Regardless of my own personal background, I was required to develop the capacity to view difficult issue from a central and elevated position. Centrality is important because it allows me to consider the range of responses that might come from the extreme positions that others will hold on an issue. Centrality keeps me from being pulled too strongly in any given direction on a potentially polarizing issue. Staying in the center puts me in the best place from which to be accessible to those who are interested in engaging in conversations about a problem. The more I stray from the center, the more distance I put between myself and some community members and the more aligned I become with some particular viewpoint. The key for me has been to find a position that is easily accessible to the community, however extreme I sometimes find their positions.

The importance of assuming an elevated position on controversial issues is to be able to raise the issue above the chaos that typically surrounds such incidents. When a polarizing event occurs on my campus it is important that I am capable of thinking about the issue in its fullness and then elevating the issue in a way that puts questions of education and community at the heart of the community discourse. If I am pulled too deeply into the middle and if I get caught amidst the chaos and clamor, then effective leadership of the situation will be made even more difficult. For this reason I have felt it is important that I possess the demeanor and outlook to elevate myself and the issue above the noise so that I can function as an effective leader and community builder.

Though I agree with DuBois that "nobody can live in the middle all the time," my experience has suggested to me that the middle is where I needed to learn to live. For it is in the middle that I have been best positioned to use the core skills of our profession and most effectively advance my institutions. From the middle I can best facilitate needed interactions, convene important conversations, bridge relationship gulfs, and hear the multiple voices of my colleagues and community members. It has been during those times that I have been most effective at "managing the middle" and elevating issues in ways that allow them to be seen and heard with greater clarity that I have been most effective as a leader.

Larry Roper's thesis is extraordinarily important in this discussion. As student affairs leaders, we manage a host of processes in which we are compelled to be fair. Personal viewpoints about the content of a dispute must be withheld until the process has worked its way along in an unbiased atmosphere. This may make the leader appear to be value neutral or even lacking values. But respecting the integrity of all who are involved demands an unbiased process and a leader who is impeccably fair. Fairness is one of the most important virtues of leadership. It is also important to remember that values don't exist in a vacuum somewhere inside us. They are connected to real people and the relationships we develop and sustain with others. And people are the ones who ultimately matter according to the values of our profession.

WILLIAM THOMAS is former vice president for student affairs at the University of Maryland–College Park.

7

The author reflects on unconventional truths that he has learned from over twenty-five years of student affairs administration.

Uncommon Truths: A Diary of Practical Wisdom

Gregory S. Blimling

As part of the research for this monograph, Jon Dalton asked a group of senior student affairs officers to share some personal reflections about their work in student affairs. This was not a difficult task for me. For many years I have kept a journal about my experiences in student affairs. I did not write in my journal every day. Instead, I wrote as a way of thinking to myself about a problem or issue with which I was struggling. I found that I became most "reflective" after I made some blunder, was forced into making some unpleasant decision, or needed an opportunity to vent. But occasionally I would just write. At Jon Dalton's request, I took some of the reflections I had written during the past twenty-five years of working in student affairs and assembled them in this chapter. I was careful to select only those items that did not embarrass me or anyone else.

The chapter is an eclectic assortment of ideas, lessons I have learned, and thoughts I have had about various subjects. It is not intended to give advice. Colleges are very different from one another. What works well in one situation at one college might not work at another. So advice is not the objective. The chapter includes only some insights I have gained through my practical experiences working in student affairs.

Going Along to Get Along Doesn't Always Work

Recently we made a decision to update our mascot. This is always a dangerous thing to do because no matter how bad the mascot is, people usually have strong feelings about it. We went about it in the right way. We hired the very best mascot consulting company in the nation, put together a committee that represented every constituent group on and off campus, and provided opportunities for input from virtually everyone on campus and off campus. The end result was a mascot that reduced everything to the lowest common denominator. No one really liked it; but because the process was good, people adopted the attitude, "I'll go along with the majority to get along."

The process seemed to work until the day the mascot was announced and shown to the student body, who had seen pictures previously. It was a disaster. They hated the mascot, thought it looked "wimpy," and it even got a few boos at a football game. The chancellor kindly suggested that we might want to rethink our results and start over.

Back to the drawing board. This time we included fewer people, gave stronger direction, and allowed the entire student body to vote on one of three options. The end result was a mascot that was more accepted and has now come to successfully represent the university. If there is a lesson I learned from this experience, it is that even when a process works, it sometimes results in a poor decision. I also learned that good decisions could be made bad when a committee reduces issues to the lowest common denominator. Finally, I learned that going along to get along doesn't always work. Occasionally you need to stand up and say, "This isn't going right."

If You Don't Know What Students Want, Ask

I am often amazed in my conversations with other administrators how often we assume we know what students want, think, or need. Occasionally we're right, but more often than not, we're not totally right. What I've learned is that if you want to know what students think, ask them. Because of this philosophy, we now do almost monthly telephone surveys with students on a variety of topics. When I don't know what students want, I ask the students through surveys. I also get input from the student government association and similar groups, but the information from the surveys I find to be a much more revealing way of knowing what students want, think, and need. It's easier to get a decision right when you have the information you need.

Adult Conversations

As institutions have grown larger, I have noticed that students have fewer "adult" conversations. If most of the conversations students are having are with their peers, their behavior and thinking—at least for traditionally aged college students—will tend to be somewhat adolescent. Don't discount the value of the adult conversation with students. It is something they need in order to grow into the adults we want them to become.

Apologizing Is Part of the Job

Never argue with angry parents. Listen and let them vent. After they have said their piece, give them the facts and apologize for anything that went wrong. Part of your job as an administrator is to apologize for the institution when it made a mistake and when it didn't.

Some Battles Aren't Worth Fighting

I recently visited a friend of mine who is the academic dean at a large research university on the West Coast. He is one of the most successful administrators I know, and part of what makes him successful is that he chooses which issues to expend his energy on and he ignores the rest. In the course of a conversation, he shared with me a series of issues that had been brought to his attention. Although he had rather strong views on a number of these, he elected not to argue or engage in trying to stop, hinder, or delay a particular issue. Instead, he simply listened and moved on with his work. He told me he had learned a valuable lesson in his life and that was that there are some battles that aren't worth fighting. If you try to fight them all, you will expend your energy and time in too many directions so that when the truly important things need to be addressed, you won't have the resources or social capital to accomplish them.

Even Legends Fade with Time

A number of years ago, I replaced a man who had served the university for over forty years as the dean of men. He was a legend at the institution; and for the first year I was there, I heard many stories about his accomplishments. He was a kind and generous man and I regret not having known him better. The second year, I heard fewer of the stories, and by the end of four years I almost never heard his name again. I learned a valuable lesson by this. Never let the authority that you have as a vice chancellor or dean let you forget that you will be forgotten a few years after you leave the position. Loyal colleagues will always be loyal; but when you leave, they will share that loyalty with another person. One of the remarkable things about working at a university is that as you grow older, students remain the same age and many of their issues remain the same although they find different ways to discuss them.

Students' Interests and Needs Are What Matter in Higher Education

Faculty will never understand student affairs work, and it doesn't really matter if they do. Occasionally they will think student affairs needs to be reorganized under academic affairs because they see themselves at the center of knowledge. Times change. People and history make organizations run, not arbitrary functional alignments. Students would learn more if colleges were organized around students' needs and interests rather than that of faculty. We also spend a lot of time talking about how students are important, but the truth is that most universities are organized around faculty needs and academic departments. It would be interesting to see what would happen if we really did organize classes and the operation of the institution around our students.

Universities Are Peculiar Places for Peculiar People

People who enter administration are an eclectic assortment drawn from a peculiar pool of people who have spent much of their time in the company of other peculiar people. Please don't assume that "peculiar" is a bad term; it's not. Higher education is a home for the nicest, brightest, and most interesting people one could meet and, at the same time, a refuge for a gaggle of eccentric, bizarre, and odd people. I have come to believe that colleges must be society's answer to a modern Noah's Ark—two of every kind. Where else could you find a serious discussion about whether or not a male teacher should be able to cross-dress as a woman while teaching class or a committee formed to work on rules to detail the circumstances under which teachers can have amorous relationships with their students? Where else could you have a required meeting for faculty that only half attend? Universities are, indeed, a peculiar place.

The Value of Students' Learning by Doing

Last night I attended one of many student banquets I attend every year. This banquet was for students who had organized a regional conference for student residence hall associations. I was not asked to be a speaker. I was just a guest who had the opportunity to sit and observe students who organized and conducted the entire meeting, including the presentation of some twenty-three separate awards. As you would expect, the evening was full of short speeches by people about what they learned from the experience of organizing this conference, the value of the friendships they formed, and how proud they were of the students with whom they worked. I was struck by the great emotions that students expressed toward one another. Crying and hugging were the commonplace exchanges among students as they talked about one another and presented various forms of recognition.

One of the things that was remarkable about this dinner was that the students were celebrating the accomplishment of putting on a workshop, which lasted two days. Most student affairs professionals would have organized the workshop themselves in a couple of weeks. These students took almost a year to organize this conference. It took weekly meetings and an array of organizational schemes to keep people in touch with what was happening. The simple process of organizing this event had a dramatic impact on the self-confidence, leadership, and feeling of accomplishment demonstrated by all the students. If I ever doubted how the experiences outside the classroom influence student learning, my doubts were obliterated last night when I saw the pride that each student took in his or her accomplishment and heard in great detail what each learned through the experience of participating.

$E = MC^2$

Recently we had an event on campus that caused more publicity than it deserved. I found that much of my time was engaged in trying to deal with the media in a positive way but to no avail. I learned some lessons from this and from some similar kinds of encounters. First, I learned that it is not a story when the university does something right. The real story is what people don't like about the university's decision even though the reasons may lack substance. Most important, I learned what I call the $E = MC^2$ principle. Simply put, the amount of energy (E) that goes into any crisis (C) is compounded by the amount of media (M) interested in that crisis. In other words, energy equals media interest in any crisis squared. Generally speaking, if I never talk to the media again, it would be too soon. Media people are mostly interested in something sensational, and I don't trust sensational journalism.

A friend of mine once told me that one must always remember that newspaper are in business to sell advertising. If they happen to get the news right, that's OK too. But remember, it's not the main purpose of having a newspaper.

A Taxonomy of College Faculty

College faculty comprise four types: (1) sincerely committed teachers who enjoy students and work at quality teaching; (2) researchers driven by the need to know, curiosity, and the love of learning; (3) careerists-entrepreneurs driven by self-interest and personal monetary goals; and (4) complainers, twaddelizers, and administrative wannabes. The first two types compose the vast majority of faculty. The last two types cause the most problems and are the source of most of the criticism about higher education.

Operating a Public University

I am amazed at how often I read articles in the newspaper about how universities could be run better or hear reports of various legislators who have championed proposals to hold universities more accountable. Most of these people are convinced that universities would run better if they were more like businesses that they understood. Despite their lack of information, most are convinced that they could do a better job. I have found that it's much easier to run a university when you don't know how, but very difficult when you do. If people had the whole truth about the details of higher education, they would give it overwhelming support. People don't have the time to invest in learning the whole truth, and complicated discussions don't always translate into editorials, fifteen-second sound bites, or cocktail conversations.

Administrators Must Renew Their Credibility Each Day with Students and Around Each Crisis

Last year we had an alleged rape that resulted in media coverage and became the impetus for some students to march and demonstrate. The details of the situation were such that no one could determine whether or not a rape had actually occurred, but the details were confidential and only the allegation was before the public. In conversations with various groups on this topic, I was surprised that there was a sense of distrust in the administration by some students. This distrust was so uncharacteristic of our student body and so out of context with how sensitive the university is to these issues that I could not understand why students did not accept the honest and candid information we tried to provide. Then I had a conversation with a new staff member who reminded me of something that I had forgotten. She said, "You must remember that our students change every year and that the administration must renew its credibility each day with students and around each crisis. They don't know you and the other administrators as we do; and until they do, they will trust other people whom they know better."

As part of this conversation, I also learned that administrators talk in terms of logic, reason, and analysis. They are logical thinkers and analytic reasoners. Sometimes they don't hear students who talk from feelings. I know from my own conversations that I often have to stop and hear students who talk from feelings even though these feelings may not have a basis in fact or logic.

The Influence of a National Peer Norm on College Student Culture

Several years ago I had an opportunity to participate in a Fulbright program in Germany. While waiting for a train one day, I noticed a group of twelve- to fourteen-year-old boys riding skateboards. They were wearing football jerseys and long baggy pants popular in the United States, had their baseball hats on backwards, and had a boom box playing rap music. These boys could have been on any street in the United States, but they were Germans in a medium-sized town in Germany. It reminded me how important American pop culture is to the behaviors and attitudes of young people.

This became even more apparent in a conversation I had with a group of students in a leadership class I teach. Each fall I take this class to New York City. On the trip in the van from the airport to our accommodations last year, students began talking about the Gap commercials. Almost every one of these fifteen students could describe in great detail the music that was played in the Gap commercials, the origin of the music, and why one commercial was better than another. I do watch television occasionally, but I must admit that I was completely oblivious to the culture of the Gap commercial.

These two events made it very clear to me the dramatic influence that the national peer culture has on student attitudes, values, aspirations, and behavior. There was a time when I was younger that I watched the TV show *Saturday Night Live.* I can recall that people at that time talked about various episodes and it became part of the social milieu for the campus. MTV and various television programs serve that same function on many college campuses. Much of what students wear, the music they listen to, their vocabulary, the "inside jokes," what's cool and what's not, and a variety of other behavioral and attitudinal things are set not on our college campuses but by the national media and the peer culture.

These are not the standards set by universities or by the campus peer culture as much as by the national peer culture. Our ability to be able to affect student behavior on campus and how students act is translated through the national peer groups and pop culture. Although this may not be a revelation, it certainly changes the dynamics of how we do our job and the types of things that we should be attending to in order to influence student learning on campus.

Strategic Planning

Every two years, our division is required by a state mandate to write a five-year strategic plan. This has become more of an exercise in filling a requirement than doing real planning. Strategic planning does not work very well in higher education. Deming, in his book *Out of the Crisis* (2000 [1982]), observed that stable systems really are not capable of continued improvement. In a stable organizational system, one gets whatever the system delivers. Establishing strategic objectives and lofty goals beyond what the system can deliver is unrealistic and a waste of time.

A second problem with strategic planning is that higher education is too dynamic to do too much advanced planning. Several years ago, the state was projecting a budget surplus; now we have a deficit. How could we have planned for that? Students were killed in a residence hall fire in another state, and there is now a move afoot to retrofit older residence halls with sprinklers, costing millions of dollars, none of which was planned.

What may work is something I call *strategic positioning*. Strategic positioning is a focus on creating an infrastructure to be able to respond to the demands of a trend and to find good people who have the vision to make incremental changes when opportunities arise. I do not think of this as strategic planning. It's taking advantage of emerging opportunities. Five-year plans work great for growth organizations where one has considerable control over what goes on; they work poorly in higher education.

Responding to Student Protests and Demonstrations

We had a student protest today, not unexpected. A group of our students, concerned about using a wooded area for a new building, chained themselves to a water faucet outside the chancellor's office. They vowed to stay there until we agreed not to build the building in that location. I admire the students for having the courage to stand up for what they believe. It takes conviction to place your college career at risk. The students were nonviolent, and I knew most of them. I bought them pizza, they talked to various newspaper reporters, and eventually I talked them into leaving—once they knew their story would appear on the nightly news.

I have been in student affairs a long time and learned some things about demonstrations in the 1970s when students from Iran were protesting against the Shah. I found that I made my greatest mistakes with protests and demonstrations when I did not know the students well. The better I knew the students, the less of a confrontation there was. It is much easier to deal with students when there is a mutual sense of trust. I also learned that there has to be a balance between the university's interest in ensuring the education of students (their right to protest) and its interest in protecting its reputation. Neither one can be sacrificed.

What seems to work in dealing with these situations is to recognize the students' interest, know the students who are raising issues that are likely to result in protests and demonstrations, and facilitate their access to media outlets that allow them to be heard—although I've learned about the media the hard way. It is also to ensure that the university is not totally disrupted, people threatened, or property destroyed. Students don't have the right to occupy a building and prevent others from doing their work. In circumstances where that has happened, the event needs to end prior to the start of the next work day even if that means having to physically remove students. Although I have never reached a point where that was necessary, there are occasions in which it is the right thing to do.

Also, I do not believe in punishing students for doing what they believe is right. Occasionally, this means that certain disciplinary policies might be slightly compromised, but one needs to weigh these issues against a host of other more important student learning objectives and the administrative energy and time it takes to pursue the matter—often with questionable outcomes.

Fraternity Membership

I never joined a fraternity when I was in college. So when I was asked (at the age of thirty-four as dean of students at Louisiana State University) to become a member of a popular fraternity on campus, I was honored. Fraternities occasionally recognize the work of somebody who has helped them, by getting "special dispensation" to initiate that person as a member. One only participates in the induction ceremony, not the pledging.

The induction ceremony was quite remarkable. It required commitments of character and pledges of integrity. More important, it developed a sense of connectedness with others in the organization—a sense of bonding. I was very moved by the ceremony and the feeling of closeness that that experience produced.

I cannot imagine that undergraduate students who have this experience fail to have this same sense of connectedness and feeling of belonging after induction. What I regret most about fraternities is that the experience of being connected to others in the organization somehow gets lost in the process of socializing, partying, and harassing new pledges. For an experience that can be so positive, it is disheartening to see what it so often has become in practice.

Creating Memorable College Experiences

Student affairs has a responsibility to help create memorable college experiences for students. Traditions, rituals, mascots, and other formal and informal situations created a sense of linkage and continuity with the institution. When I was at LSU, our strongest alumni support came from the generations of students who were required to participate in ROTC as a condition of attendance at the institution. I would be among the last to advocate such a program, but it was a strong link in developing a set of common experiences for these students.

On a recent visit to the University of North Carolina–Chapel Hill campus, I could not help but notice monuments to Civil War heroes, historic buildings that had been restored, and buildings named after various national figures who had association with the institution. These symbols link students with the past, even those things in the past of which an institution may not have been proud. It is important for the heritage, traditions, and life of a campus for there to be such experiences for students; and it is part of student affairs' job to make sure that they exist and are transmitted and that students feel a sense of belonging to the university through them.

Investing in Research

At an annual social event for the State Treasurer's office held on our campus, I sat next to a CEO from a well-known investment company. He invested about a billion dollars of the state's money, and he was extraordinarily successful at it. I asked him what he thought was most important to him in evaluating a company in which to invest. What he said was, "I invest in companies that have made major investments in research. These companies know more about what's happening, make better decisions, and have the advantage of being ahead of the market in new products, ideas, and techniques."

If universities invested more of their resources in researching what works in student learning and what doesn't, we might be more successful. Investing in research on students is an investment in the future of our universities. It will pay dividends in student success.

Information Doesn't Change Behavior

Last week we had a student die of alcohol poisoning. Technically, he wasn't a student because he had left the university approximately a month prior to his death. But for me, he was one of our students. On his twenty-first birthday he went out with friends to drink. He died of alcohol poisoning later that evening. I have just about given up on what to do about alcohol and other drugs. We have done every conceivable program on alcohol and drugs that one can do. We have full-time people who do nothing but drug and alcohol education programs, and the data we get on alcohol consumption, binge drinking, and drug use shows that this information has absolutely no effect on changing behavior. We have tried the renorming approach, and it doesn't work. I have read the research, and much of it is speculative and, for the most part, not very well done.

It seems to me that the real goal of dealing with alcohol is to keep our students alive until the age of twenty-four. After the age of twenty-four, alcohol consumption plummets, regardless of what we do. Although I thought I would never say this, the only thing that seems to deter excessive consumption of alcohol is the likelihood that students may get caught and suffer consequences. Information doesn't change behavior. If it did, no one would smoke cigarettes. We do educational programs because it's part of what we do in student affairs and it's expected of us. But it has little effect.

I really don't mind if students drink occasionally as long as they don't kill themselves in the process, injure themselves or other people, damage property, or commit some other act of violence. The problem is that when some students drink, they drink too much and they do all the things that destroy their lives and the lives of others. I wish I had a solution, but I don't.

Conclusions

Senior student affairs officers can take a division of student affairs in the direction it is headed. Sometimes they can move it slightly one way or slightly another way, but change comes slowly and only through consensus building. By becoming part of the organization, one develops relationships and builds capital that create the opportunity for realizing opportunities. I am reasonably sure there is not a set of right and wrong answers about working in student affairs. Training and experience help, and good judgment frequently is learned by making mistakes. What has to be at the heart of every good student affairs educator is the desire to give every student the best possible undergraduate education he or she can have, and to keep the best interest of students at the center of decision making. I have found that when I do this, I almost always make better decisions. I have also learned that whatever decision I make is better if I listen to a number of other people before I make it.

In this chapter I have provided some random reflections taken from notes that I have accumulated over the past twenty-five years. This is a work in progress. I try to learn every day, and sometimes I get things right and sometimes I don't. But the longer I do the job, the less often I seem to make the same mistakes. When it is my time to leave this position, I can only hope that students will believe they had a great education at my institution and will feel good about the education they received.

Reference

Deming, W. E. *Out of the Crisis.* Cambridge: MIT Press, 2000 [1982].

GREG BLIMLING is vice chancellor for student development at Appalachian State University. He serves as editor of the Journal of College Student Development, *published by the American College Personnel Association.*

8

Long-range career planning is difficult in the student affairs profession because of the lack of clearly defined career tracks and inherent job insecurities. The authors present and discuss strategies for planning for retirement and other late career options.

Life Planning: Preparing for Transitions and Retirement

Elizabeth Nuss, Charles Schroeder

Retiring, taking late career options, knowing when you are ready to make a life transition, dealing with forced professional exits or changes, and ensuring the enduring satisfactions of a successful career are all matters that require the practical and mature wisdom Jon Dalton discussed in Chapter One. Decisions and choices on these matters require both sound knowledge and good judgment. Many student affairs professionals spend years aspiring to and preparing for the chief student affairs officer position but spend little, if any, time thinking about what position or assignment might follow this role.

This chapter will provide information for student affairs administrators to think about the issues related to retirement or the transition from the chief student affairs officer (CSAO) role. Some of the literature on adults in transition will be discussed. We draw heavily upon our conversations with the community of colleagues who have successfully experienced transitions. Their experiences and perspectives raise important issues to consider in shaping plans for retirement and other transitions. Topics covered include adult transition issues, reasons colleagues leave the CSAO role and typical next steps, financial planning, and a summary of useful lessons gleaned from our conversations with colleagues. A principal theme of this chapter is the central role that planning should play in preparing for and successfully managing transitions. As Charles Schroeder suggests in the following vignette, being intentional and planning, particularly with regard to major transitions such as retirement, are critical to success.

I have many passions in my life but none is more important than my love of the outdoors. Each year I journey to southwest Montana to spend weeks in the

Beartooth-Absaroka Primitive Area. Prior to the trip I spend countless hours reviewing topographical maps, checking the condition of my equipment, determining various "exit strategies" in case of emergencies, and developing fairly specific goals for reaching various destinations. Once I am on the trip, I rely heavily on my compass, topographical maps, equipment, preplanned routes, and my ability to adapt to unforeseen circumstances (that is, unexpected storms, swollen rivers, downed timber, forest fires, and so forth). Planning for retirement is akin to planning a wilderness expedition. The key is not to blunder into the retirement forest with no map and no idea of where you are going.

Knowing When You Are Ready to Make a Transition

At a NASPA seminar for women preparing to be chief student affairs officers, Elizabeth Nuss (1994) suggested that there was a need for senior student affairs officers to think more intentionally about their roles as an assignment rather than as a permanent position. She noted that the needs of institutions and the demands on the role change over time. It is often difficult to accurately assess whether one's leadership style is appropriate for the current challenges an institution or organization faces. In some organizations it is possible for the leader to be very versatile and facile; in others the leader has considerable flexibility in selecting assistants and department heads and can bring the required new perspectives and skills to the team. But in some instances and organizations it is important for the leaders to recognize when it is time for them to be replaced so that the most appropriate leadership skills are available for the contemporary challenges facing the institution. How do professionals know when it is time for them to consider a transition from the CSAO role to a new one? Are we able to recognize when we have outlived our usefulness to an institution or division? How do we plan for our next assignment so that we can effectively and gracefully make the transition? In the following Elizabeth Nuss shares some of her experiences about recognizing when the time for a transition may be appropriate.

> In my own case I think back to my service as NASPA executive director. In 1987 I had the right leadership style and the requisite skills to get the association established in Washington, D.C., and to launch the association in new ways. But after eight years it was increasingly apparent to me that the organization needed to be launched to the next level. It needed someone who was enthusiastic and skilled in grant writing and had a more entrepreneurial approach. Those were not things I liked to do, nor was I the best at those tasks. I concluded it was time for change with the association and me.

Adult Transition Issues

"It isn't the changes that do you in, it's the transitions" (Bridges, 1991, p. 3). Bridges notes that transition is different from change. Change is situational and external like a new boss or a new project or assignment.

Transition is the internal, psychological process people go through to come to terms with the new situation (Bridges, 1991; Reeves, 1999). Transitions are the anticipated and non-anticipated events or non-events that alter adult lives (Reeves, 1999; Sargent and Schlossberg, 1988; Schlossberg, 1984). Transitions provide individuals with the opportunity to take stock of and take charge of their lives. Transitions often begin with having to let go of something. The starting point for transition is leaving the old situation behind. The second step is the neutral zone or phase between the old and new reality. Emerging from the neutral zone means a new beginning. Individuals are typically in more than one of the zones at the same time, and the movement through transition is marked by change in the dominance of one phase as it gives way to another (Bridges, 1991). Persons in transition bring certain strengths and weaknesses to dealing with the process.

Sargent and Schlossberg (1988) outlined three basic tenets of adult behavior that are useful in thinking about adult transitions and retirement issues. They note that "adult behavior is determined by transition not age; adults are motivated to learn and to change by their continued need to belong, matter, master, renew, and take stock; and adult readiness for change depends on their situation, support, self, and strategies" (p. 58). To cope effectively with transition adults need to assess these four S's. Situation, support, and self represent the aspects of taking stock, and the fourth S, strategies, is the aspect of taking charge.

Situation. In assessing the situation one must understand the kind of situation. Is it expected or unexpected? Is it a voluntary or imposed choice? And is the individual in the beginning, middle, or end of the transition?

Self. What strengths and limitations does the individual bring to the situation? What is the person's prior experience with transitions, and how has he or she handled those situations? Prior experience can make new transitions somewhat easier.

Supports. Does the person have individuals or circumstances that will support or hinder the transition?

Strategies for coping. This is the plan of action for taking charge of the transition. How versatile is the person? Is he or she able to change the meaning of the situation or change the situation? How has he or she prepared in the past?

Cantor's (2000) book, *What Do You Want to Do When You Grow Up? Starting the Next Chapter of Your Life,* contains a variety of personal accounts and assessment exercises and questions that are very helpful in guiding a personal assessment of your individual strengths and limitations in preparing for or responding to a transition such as retirement. She notes that individuals are looking for a combination of circumstances that provide the greatest well-being in retirement. In her terms well-being requires having meaning, establishing objectives, realizing potential, being open to new experiences, and finding the right fit (Cantor, 2000).

Reasons for Leaving the CSAO Role and Typical Next Steps

There are many and varied reasons why a chief student affairs officer may decide to leave the role and move on to a different challenge. Most of the colleagues with whom we consulted said they knew when they were ready for a change. The most typical reasons cited were the crisis management and physical and emotional demands of the job, a sense of solving the same problems again, less patience or enthusiasm for problem solving, or a sense that they had accomplished what they could at the institution.

Some colleagues chose to move to another CSAO assignment at a different type of institution or to an institution located in a different part of the country. Some aspired to become college presidents; others were interested in roles as faculty members or in other administrative assignments. Some considered part-time assignments, others sought roles outside of higher education, and some indeed retired in the more traditional sense of the word. In some cases the individual had planned and prepared for the transition and in other cases it was prompted by institutional needs or other circumstances not necessarily in the individual's control.

The key point is many colleagues have effectively transitioned from the CSAO position under a variety of circumstances. The successful and meaningful next step depends, however, on the individual's prior experiences and successes. In many cases, institutional type and culture also play an important role. The most successful CSAOs are both exceptional leaders of the student affairs division and influential members of the institutional governance team. They are trusted as leaders who have a keen sense of the overall institutional priorities and needs. As a result, they often have experiences and have developed important relationships with students, faculty, trustees, influential alumnae, friends, and donors; many have served on local, regional, or national community boards or served in key roles in professional associations. These experiences and relationships often lead to the meaningful next step.

For example, colleagues who remain at colleges and universities with experience teaching in either undergraduate or graduate programs may become faculty members, those with long-standing relationships with former students may move into alumni affairs and development work, and others may serve as secretary to the board of trustees. A dean at a midwestern urban institution served as a volunteer member of the board of directors for a community foundation for several years. When the foundation was creating a position for an executive director, the dean was tapped for the role. Another retired vice president was appointed as executive director of her national professional association. Others have assumed leadership for national fraternity and sororities, continued a private counseling practice, consulted with colleges and universities and other organizations, managed community associations, or continued their ongoing volunteer work with Habitat for Humanity or other community service organizations.

Some of the personal observations from colleagues provide some perspectives to consider. "The academic culture instills in us a sense that once one is in higher education that it is somehow demeaning to leave it; but there is more to life than that and there are many personally fulfilling and rewarding paths to take. Fulfill your own needs and dreams, not those of traditional culture; sort out your own values from what might be peer pressure" (C. DeRemer, personal communication, 2001).

> After thirty-one years as CSAO, I left the position because the president asked me to serve as senior vice president. If I had been thirty years old I am sure my present position would have been called "assistant to the president.". . . About 30 percent of my time was spent as a consultant to the WSU Foundation, 30 percent on direct assignments from the president, and the remainder doing whatever needed to be done on behalf of the university. . . . I had thought about my eventual transition from the vice president's role. For most of my life I felt that at sixty-five I would seek a half-time job in University College, a freshman unit on campus. I saw this as a way to play to the strengths in my background. I did not anticipate, until the day it happened, the offer from the president to join him in his suite and attend to the business that he identified needing attention. (J. Rhatigan, personal communication, 2001)

"This is a difficult decision. I love my work at Goucher but must consider my desire and need for more flexible time with my family. I have so many mixed feelings. Relief came after months of consideration, talking with family and friends, and worrying about the uncertainties. The decision is finally made and announced. No more feeling like I am being less than honest with my colleagues. I feel good about what I have accomplished, but there is so much more to do. Five years is a short time in an institutional history" (Elizabeth Nuss).

"I am pleased that I made my planned transition to the faculty and that I was able to do it on my terms, at a time when my work was viewed positively by my colleagues in student affairs and administration. I have witnessed too many friends and colleagues who have been forced out of their senior student affairs positions, and with the politics of institutions being so volatile these days, I was fortunate to make my move when I did. It is always best, if possible, to move when one is still wanted" (Arthur Sandeen).

Forced Professional Exits

Admittedly, CSAOs who experience an unexpected and forced professional exit often have more difficulty in the transition. In most cases, the action is not the result of malfeasance in office but rather as a result of a change in institutional priorities or leadership style. It happens to all senior officers, not just student affairs officers. Senior officers in development, financial affairs, or student affairs typically do not have tenure in an academic department as the provost or vice president for academic affairs has. The NASPA publication *Involuntary Termination: What If It Happens to You?* (NASPA, 1991) provides a wealth of practical and highly relevant information on how to deal with the many difficult challenges associated with involuntary separation. For many CSAOs this is, without a doubt, one of the most challenging issues they will face in their career. This challenge requires a host of responses often involving legal, psychological, financial, spiritual, and other resources.

Retirement

Retirement stands as one of the most important economic, psychological, and social transitions in most people's lives (Aaron, 1999; Arkin, 1998). As life expectancies and incomes rise, people are spending more time in retirement or new roles. Retirement in America takes many different routes. For many Americans retirement is a process, not a single event. Many use one or more transitional or bridge jobs between career employment and complete withdrawal from the labor force (Quinn and Kozy, 1996). Since the 1970s people work increasingly often in new part-time roles or are self-employed after they leave their career jobs. The literature suggests that retirees return to work for many reasons. Some miss the structure and social interactions that the job provides and others find their financial resources to be inadequate (Mergenhagen, 1994).

Retirement is typically an active, rewarding period for most adults. It is characterized by time to pursue new interests or complete tasks they had to postpone or devote less time to during their working years. Retirees are typically satisfied individuals who retain a sense of usefulness and pride in themselves and their accomplishments. However, it is not a pleasant experience for all. Retirees with financial problems, health issues, whose identity was tied up in their jobs, who were forced to retire, and who have made few, if any, plans often have trouble adjusting (Arkin, 1998). Whether people are able to adjust satisfactorily depends to a large extent on the attitudes and behavior patterns developed during their working years. Arkin (1998) concludes that to make a good adjustment, people must be willing to reorganize their lives and change their self-perspective.

Financial Planning

It is not surprising that financial issues are typically the ones people focus on first when considering retirement. There are some very good reasons for this but this chapter stresses that finances are only one of the issues or supports that an individual must assess in either making the determination to retire or in coping with a career change. There are many excellent materials available from major financial service companies such as TIAA-CREF, Fidelity, Vanguard, and Merrill Lynch, to name but a few. In addition, a tremendous amount of useful and relevant information is on the Web at sites such as fidelity.com, troweprice.com, financeware.com, and zunna.com. A few strategies most appropriate for educators and chief student affairs officers to consider are outlined here.

As Charles Schroeder noted earlier, planning for retirement is akin to planning and implementing a wilderness expedition. The key is not to blunder into the retirement forest with no map and no idea of where you are going. Successful retirement planning starts with some fundamental questions: How much money will I have when I retire? How much will I need each year when I am retired? Can I retire early? How do I want to live in retirement—travel, spend time with my family, learn new hobbies, start a second career? What unexpected challenges might I face—the need to support aging parents who must have extended health care or support (God forbid) adult children who decide to move back home?

Charles Schroeder writes:

These are but a few issues that I have struggled with over the years as I have thought about an eventual reality—retirement. Unfortunately, neither my parents nor my formal schooling ever addressed the issue of planning for retirement. Nonetheless, this has been one area of my life where I feel that I have excelled. A story that I heard over twenty years ago is a part of my success in retirement.

This story goes something like this. A young man and his family traveled to Florida for a relatively brief summer vacation. They drove their car and pop-up trailer into a state park and started to set up camp. Because the father was having difficulty setting up the trailer, he went to the next campsite and asked an older man to help him. He noticed that the older man was driving a Cadillac and towing an Airstream trailer. As they assembled the pop-up tent camper, the younger man asked the older one what he did for a living. The man replied that he was "retired." Because the older man appeared to be in his early fifties, the younger man was perplexed. "How old are you?" he asked. The man replied, "Fifty-two." "How in the world did you retire at such an early age—did you win the lottery?" the younger man asked. With a smile, the older man replied, "No. . . . I simply paid myself first." The younger man responded, "What do you mean, you paid yourself first?" "Well," the older man replied, "I did a relatively simple thing. Each month, when I got my paycheck, instead of paying all of my bills first and then hoping I had enough left over to put in a savings account, I reversed the process. The first check I wrote was initially to a passbook savings account. When I reached my goal, I then started buying shares in mutual funds, then individual stocks and bonds, real estate, various tax shelters, etc. Over the last thirty years, the cumulative effects of these investments have enabled me to live the lifestyle I want to live at an early age."

There are a lot of lessons that can be learned from this story. First, successful retirement planning must be a priority and, to a degree, a lifelong process. Starting early makes all the difference in the world. For example, small, consistent contributions to tax-deferred plans such as a 403B or 401K that compound tax-free will produce phenomenal results over a thirty to forty-year period. For instance, if you contributed $5,000 annually for thirty years to a 401(k) plan, you would wind up with $611,729 before taxes, assuming an 8 percent annual rate of return. However, the same investment taxed each year at 28 percent would leave you with only $288,587. Second, like the older man in the previous story, it is absolutely essential to develop your own financial plan complete with goals, implementation strategies, and a systematic evaluation mechanism. If you do not have the expertise to develop the plan yourself, then seek out the advice of a professional financial planner or a faculty member on your campus that teaches consumer economics and financial planning. Third, be sure to monitor your plan frequently—not every day but at least every quarter. Make adjustments in your investments as appropriate. Fourth, be sure not to put all of your eggs in one basket—diversify your assets across a broad range of investment options. And, fifth, like the older man in the preceding story, start your retirement planning journey by investing in totally safe and secure funds (certificates of deposit, money-market funds, and so forth). Create a "safety net" or "rainy day fund" of at least three to six months of salary that you could immediately access in case of an emergency. Finally, have an exit strategy. Plan for the unexpected such as a serious illness, loss of a job, or financial crisis.

Because life expectancies have increased dramatically, planning for retirement is more important today than it was thirty to forty years ago. The key to a satisfying and fulfilling retirement is financial security, and ensuring financial security requires the same kind of planning, diligence, discipline, and vigilance as needed for a successful expedition into the wilds of Montana. Since experts estimate that most retirees will need 80 percent of their final salary in order to retire comfortably, the key is to start early and follow a disciplined, meticulous process of "paying yourself first."

Serving as a senior institutional officer is an inherently risky business since the vice president or dean often serves with little, if any, job security. In preparing this chapter we sought to gain the perspectives of former CSAOs who have left the role in the past several years. We intentionally sought the perspectives of those who left the role less recently and who might have completed their transition. From these responses and the literature we have gleaned some practical advice and perhaps some wisdom to summarize.

The Importance of Planning and Preparation

Jon Dalton writes: "It pays to think long range when planning for late career transitions and retirement. The years go quickly and there are wonderful options in academe for those student affairs staff who begin to prepare early."

Jim Ratigan writes:

> It is useful to think about your retirement long before you intend to do any-thing about it. It will help you be more attentive to your contacts and your skills. You may begin to think differently about your institution, the issues it faces, and how you can help it achieve its goals. I might have left student affairs earlier if I had known more about the fundraising business and what a good transition it would be for me. My work in student affairs was so rewarding that I never looked beyond it.
>
> Plan, but plan quietly. Once it is widely known that you are thinking about retirement you may lose the influence necessary to do the job effectively.

Do It Your Way. "Making a major transition is an individual process and it is hard to generalize. Force yourself to think 'outside the box.' Be honest with yourself and think about opportunities that you might have dreamed about in the back of your mind. Don't limit your horizon to traditional goals—create your own. You have acquired quite a toolbox of experiences and skills; don't be afraid to use them" (C. DeRemer).

Consider the Implications for Family Members. Charles Schroeder writes:

> Being a senior institutional leader, particularly a CSAO, puts you in the center of institutional activity. Your lifestyle as well as your family's literally revolves around institutional expectations and commitments from football games to alumni functions to student organization events to weekly evening commitments. Retirement and other transitions can have as great or greater impact on spouse and others as they have on the CSAO. For example, transitioning from a CSAO role to a faculty role on the same campus entails shifting from the center of institutional activity with all the commitments, fanfare, and attention to a radically different lifestyle with few, if any, of the same ingredients. Spouses and other family members must adjust their lifestyles to fit the new situation and circumstances, thus creating a whole new set of challenges.

Timing. Charles Schroeder writes: "Retirement is not specifically age-related except toward the end of a career. People can make transitions at fifty, fifty-five, sixty, and so forth, and can move in many different directions. Yet as the years pass, it is inevitable that we must think about allowing a new generation of administrators to have their crack at things. I believe the aspiration should be to have people say, 'Gosh, why is she retiring?' before they say, 'Isn't he ever going to give it up?'"

Financial Planning Is Important. Elizabeth Nuss writes: "Persons who become so dependent on the larger salaries and the 'perks' associated with some senior institutional officer positions may find it more difficult to make an easy transition. It is clear that in all change something is gained and something is lost."

Charles Schroeder writes: "Expect that you might have some interruptions in your employment. Create a safety net of at least three to six months of salary that you could immediately access in case of an emergency or reduced compensation."

Develop Broad Skills. "Always be prepared for something new. Don't let the rewards of yesterday and today narrowly define you. The future is so dependent on your accepting a lifelong learning philosophy and understanding the ever-changing nature of yourself, your family, the profession, and your institution" (Don Adams).

Jon Dalton writes: "I enjoyed writing and applied research and started early to publish an occasional piece. I volunteered to teach as an adjunct faculty member and did this whenever I could at no pay. Gradually I began to think about the possibility of gaining a teaching appointment and tenure in a higher education program and I was able to do this midway through my career at Florida State University."

Being Fired Is Not the End of the World

Painful? Yes! Unfair? Maybe! But it happens. Most CSAOs know someone who was asked to leave a position for a variety of reasons. Being prepared for an unexpected transition and following the suggestions outlined in this chapter can make the situation manageable and even productive.

Make a Graceful Exit

M. Anderson writes: "Never allow yourself to succumb to the belief that you are the 'position' you hold. You must understand that all good things come to an end and that satisfaction can be had in knowing you have done a good job. Understand fully that when you leave the position it is very likely that things will change and that even some of your most cherished accomplishments may go by the board. Remember that is it no longer your job or your responsibility and that you also made changes when you first took over this job."

References

Aaron, H. J. *Behavioral Dimensions of Retirement Economics*. Washington, D.C.: Brookings Institution Press, 1999.

Arkin, L. R. *Human Development in Adulthood*. New York: Plenum, 1998.

Bridges, W. *Managing Transitions: Making the Most of Change*. Reading, Mass.: Addison-Wesley, 1991.

Cantor, D. *What Do You Want to Do When You Grow Up? Starting the Next Chapter of Your Life*. New York: Little, Brown, 2000.

Mergenhagen, P. "Rethinking Retirement." *American Demographics*, 1996, 16(6), 28–34.

National Association of Student Personnel Administrators (NASPA). *Involuntary Termination: What If It Happens to You?* Washington, D.C.: NASPA, 1991.

Nuss, E. "Preparing to be a Chief Student Affairs Officer," NASPA Seminar for Women, Washington, D.C., 1994.
Quinn, J. F., and Kozy, M. "The Role of Bridge Jobs in the Retirement Transition: Gender, Race, and Ethnicity." *The Gerontologist,* 1996, 36(3), 363–372.
Reeves, P. M. "Psychological Development: Becoming a Person." In M. C. Clark and R. S. Cafferella (eds.), *Update on Adult Development Theory: New Ways of Thinking About the Life Course.* New Directions for Adult and Continuing Education, no. 84. San Francisco: Jossey-Bass, 1999.
Sargent, A., and Schlossberg, N. K. "Managing Adult Transitions." *Training & Development Journal,* 1988, 42(12), 58–60.
Schlossberg, N. K. *Counseling Adults in Transition.* New York: Springer Publishing, 1984.

ELIZABETH NUSS is former vice president and dean of students at Goucher College. She served previously as executive director of the National Association of Student Personnel Administrators.

CHARLES SCHROEDER is former vice chancellor for student affairs at University of Missouri in Columbia and serves as "special consultant to the chancellor" and adjunct faculty in the department of education.

9

The authors offer a compilation of maxims, advice, and anecdotes that convey some essential truths they have learned about professional leadership in student affairs.

Nuggets of Practical Wisdom

Jon C. Dalton, Alicia Trexler

Every fall students flock to the Student Union plaza at Florida State University to sort through large selections of colorful posters for sale. The most popular ones are a combination of pictures and poems or sayings. The words used on posters are most often in the form of a quote or phrase that conveys an inspirational thought or truth. I have watched this annual ritual for many years and have often wondered about the attraction that words and visual images on posters have for college students.

Freshmen appear to be the most frequent buyers. Perhaps the posters have a unique appeal to the special blend of restless expectation and idealism that new students seem to feel at the beginning of their college experience. Quotes and sayings are so popular with college students that many keep quote books in which they record their favorite nuggets of wisdom (Toor, 2001, p. B13). The posters usually wind up in students' dorm or apartment rooms and serve as reminders about some special truth or inspiration that touches them in a personal way. For the young, quotes and sayings serve as inspiring guideposts for the unexplored future; they are personal cheerleaders and motivators for the unknown challenges and experiences that lie ahead. Quotes and sayings represent what one might call "nuggets" of practical wisdom. They convey important truths about life that guide decision making and provide a framework of meaning. For college students these nuggets of truth most often come from others, since their own life experiences are usually quite limited.

For older individuals, more tested and honed by life's sharper edges, nuggets of practical wisdom are also popular, but they play a somewhat different role. They are drawn more often from individuals' own experience and represent the enduring residue of what has worked and remained true for them over a lifetime. Moreover, they also serve as a core of meaning and truth that reflects the essence of an individual's beliefs and values. If students continually add to a growing collection of nuggets of practical wisdom in quote books, older persons are usually more inclined to do just the opposite: to winnow and refine their nuggets of wisdom until a relatively few remain that have weathered the test of time and experience.

Maxims and sayings have long been popular as guides to daily living and reminders about what is enduring and meaningful in life. They are the bedrock of beliefs and values that form the basis of personal character and wisdom. The nuggets of practical wisdom we present in this chapter represent some of the enduring truths about being a professional that the volume authors have identified through the crucible of their own experience. Although we believe that all professionals must discover for themselves their own credo of enduring truths, there can be great value in learning from the wisdom gained from others.

Simple Truths: Basic Nuggets of Practical Wisdom

Authors were asked to identify some basic truths they had learned through their long experience as student affairs professionals and to write these truths in short summary statements or, as we shall refer to them, *nuggets* of practical wisdom. These nuggets represent the essence of what the authors feel is most important and enduring about their life's work in student affairs. We have not attempted to prioritize their summaries, nor are they intended to represent all of the important beliefs and convictions of the authors.

The nuggets of practical wisdom in this chapter are presented in different forms. Some are short quotes or maxims. Some are mini-essays in which the authors summarize their convictions on key professional issues. Others are statements of advice. All the nuggets share a common style of succinctness and focused reflection about important personal and professional truths.

The Student Affairs Profession

Arthur Sandeen reflects on the essential work of student affairs and what has meant most to him as a professional.

> Student affairs is a wonderful and rewarding profession. I can't think of a better way to spend one's career.
> Administrative hassles and campus politics are quickly forgotten. What lasts is what is best—personal relationships with students.
> Semi-autonomous fiefdoms now dominate our campuses, making the creation of a true sense of community more difficult than ever. This means an even more important role for student affairs.
> The quality of young people entering the profession is the best it has ever been, and the quality of the graduate teaching faculty is also the best it has

been. Nevertheless, new ideas and fresh approaches to our work are needed.

Technology is dazzling and mesmerizing. But student affairs' main agenda is not efficient service; it is leadership, interpersonal relations, values, and effective service.

There is no prescription for leadership; it comes in different shapes and sizes, depending on the person and the institution. The trick is to find the right fit.

The growing amount and quality of empirical research about student learning and development is very useful; however, student affairs is not a science, and our best work still has to do more with compassion than anything else.

As the profession has rapidly developed, especially in the past forty years, it has succumbed to the same specialization that has plagued other fields. There are now over thirty national professional associations in student affairs. The most powerful and important concept in the field—the education of the whole student—should not be lost.

It is too easy to become one's job—to define oneself as a position. This is dangerous. The healthiest people have their own identity, not dependent upon any job, and will be the same person whether a plumber or a dean.

Life is very short; having the chance to work in a field one can believe in helps make it worthwhile.

Moral Choices in Leadership Roles

Larry Roper's nuggets of practical wisdom focus especially on standards of personal and professional integrity and provide helpful insights on leadership effectiveness. As an African American professional, Larry also provides some important observations on the wisdom he has learned about dealing with diversity issues as a leader.

Don't be a token. I won't let my presence take the heat off the organization to achieve greater diversity or have others represent institutional perspectives on diversity.

Develop a set of high personal principles. The principles that guide my professional engagement must focus on doing "what's right." It is important to me to not get trapped in situations where I am fighting for someone just because of their race or some other factor that has little to do with the truth.

Make clear the values that will define my presence and involvement. I will have clarity about why I am there and what I am seeking to accomplish.

Stay clear of emotional arguments. It is important for me know the facts and use them as the basis for my stances. I work hard to not expose my "hot buttons" and to not let others have access to them.

Maintain perspective. I try to keep my ego on the shelf. I should not take every negative behavior by another person as a personal threat. Not every situation is a win-lose proposition. Just because another person is looking for a fight, I don't have to give them one. Stay humble.

Have a set of personal standards and keep them high. I will always be my own harshest critic. Don't accept shallow praise. I need to know when I have not achieved a high standard.

Be selective in the battles in which I become involved. Ask myself these important questions before I become involved. Does a threat exist? What am I fighting for and is it worth a fight? Are the results worth it? What will success look and feel like to me?

Be cautious about invoking charges of racism often. Be clear about what racism is and how I can evaluate when it is a factor. Don't accept or live down to the stereotypes that others might hold about me.

Have a plan for your personal growth and development—take that plan seriously. No one should or will ever take my life, my dreams, or my growth more seriously than me.

Maintain balance in my life. Be sure to take time for myself to do the things that make me feel most alive. Stay physically, emotionally, psychologically, and spiritually healthy.

Tell the truth to others and myself. People may question my racial loyalty, but never give them cause to question my integrity. Keep in mind that loyalty to a person or an institution comes at a cost. Be loyal to myself. Don't sacrifice myself or allow myself to be sacrificed.

Don't stay anywhere too long!

Blunders of Student Affairs Administration

Student affairs professionals learn practical wisdom through both positive and negative experiences. Sometimes the mistakes or blunders one makes can serve as the most powerful teacher. In this section Greg Blimling identifies nuggets of practical wisdom that are conveyed through the common mistakes made by student affairs leaders. Greg's thoughtful approach to practical wisdom juxtaposes important professional roles or responsibilities with missing values or competencies. What is missing represents an essential truth that cannot be ignored if one is to be successful as a professional.

Administration without compassion
Leadership without knowledge
Instruction without caring
College without community
Teaching without respect
Intellect without character
Programming without enthusiasm
Services without learning
Authority without stewardship
Prestige without substance

Essential Traits of a Successful Student Affairs Administrator

At the time of Bud (William) Thomas's retirement in 2001 he was asked to reflect on some of the practical wisdom he had learned from his more than twenty-five years as vice provost for student affairs at the University of Maryland. These are some of his nuggets of practical wisdom.

> A leader must be there; you are supposed to be there.
>
> Be good at what you do.
>
> Accumulate power. *Power* is a word that gets abused a lot, but it's the best word to get your attention.
>
> If you don't have stature, you don't get listened to.
>
> Never hire anybody who's not better at what you want them to do than you could ever be.
>
> Make a habit of surrounding yourself with people who are far, far better than you are.

We suggest that one way to use the maxims of this chapter is as part of a self-guided reflection on values and ethics in professional leadership. The conclusions you draw about the enduring truths that have guided your professional practice may be different from those identified by the authors, but their convictions about practical wisdom may help you on your way.

Reference

Toor, R. "Commonplaces: From Quote Books to 'Sig' Files." *Chronicle of Higher Education,* May 25, 2001, p. B13.

JON C. DALTON *is associate professor of higher education and director of the Center for the Study of Values in College Student Development at Florida State University.*

ALICIA TREXLER *is a second-year higher education master's student at Florida State University in the department of educational leadership.*

10

The authors offer concluding observations and recommendations on using practical wisdom in professional practice.

Concluding Thoughts

Jon C. Dalton, Marguerite McClinton

Practical wisdom is the ability to draw upon knowledge in a selective manner and to apply it in fitting ways in the practical situations that arise in the course of professional work. Practical wisdom is gained through a combination of knowledge and experience in which the ability to discern what is appropriate in any given situation is guided by sound knowledge and good judgment. We believe that practical wisdom is, in the end, an art. It is cultivated through experience, reflective practice, and seasoning of the soul. Like any art, practical wisdom in the student affairs profession can be governed only by broad principles, since its practice is always an act of creative expression by each individual.

Practical wisdom is an art of skilled leadership that comes from repeated execution of professional tasks over significant time. When a student affairs leader has dealt with problems and issues on a daily basis over many years and has managed to be successful most of the time, there comes a growing confidence that the underlying truth and meaning in situations can be discerned very early. Practical wisdom permits one to imagine and foresee the likely outcomes of situations and make early interventions to avoid undesirable outcomes. Sharon Parks describes wisdom as embodying "a deep conviction of truth" (Parks, 2001, p. 60). Practical wisdom embodies a deep conviction about what will and will not work in given situations based on accumulated experience and reflection.

Long-term success in student affairs leadership requires the development of practical wisdom. As one moves to higher levels of leadership the increasing span of responsibilities brings more complex problems and a wider array of issues. Student affairs leaders must be able to solve more problems and solve them more quickly. Practical wisdom is one of the most

New Directions for Student Services, no. 98, Summer 2002 © Wiley Periodicals, Inc.

critical leadership skills for diagnosing and resolving problems more efficiently. Because it enables leaders to recognize the truth and meaning of problem situations early and resolve them more quickly, practical wisdom enables leaders to manage a broader range of issues and increasingly complex problems.

Practical wisdom often appears to the observer as gifted intelligence or special talent; in most cases, however, it is a practical skill developed through repeated experience and reflection. In other words, practical wisdom can be learned by student affairs professionals. Of course there is no complete substitute for experience, but the learning process can be accelerated through study and reflection on the accumulated practical wisdom of mentors and role models.

Since change constantly redefines the tasks of leadership in student affairs, practical wisdom must also change and adapt to new tasks, new knowledge, and new meanings. This is one reason practical wisdom cannot be static and codified. It cannot be collected as a textbook and studied as a science. Its essence is to some extent always personal, testimonial, and anecdotal. Its lessons are always shaped by present circumstances and realities. Consequently, the power of practical wisdom is best conveyed through the testimonies of individuals. It is through their personal stories and insights that professional artistry is shared and transmitted.

We have also argued that there is an enduring quality of practical wisdom and that it can serve to provide direction and content to what is good and essential about student affairs leadership. This is not a contradictory claim to what has been argued previously. Practical wisdom provides guideposts that help us find the way toward enduring truths that give lasting meaning to the work we do. Guideposts help point the way, but each one of us makes the journey our own way and creates our own special meaning in the context of the shared experiences and wisdom of others. We hope this monograph provides some valuable guideposts for those who seek to deepen their understanding of the student affairs profession and the special challenges of leadership.

We are grateful to the student affairs leaders who contributed to this special volume. Their stories and reflections, told with great candor and genuineness, help us better understand the practical wisdom of the profession we have chosen for our life's work. We hope their insights and personal convictions about the work of student affairs leadership will be useful to practitioners, graduate students, and graduate faculty in better understanding and facilitating the development of practical wisdom in the profession.

Reference

Parks, S. *Big Questions, Worthy Dreams.* San Francisco: Jossey-Bass, 2001.

JON C. DALTON *is associate professor of higher education and director of the Center for the Study of Values in College Student Development at Florida State University.*

MARGUERITE MCCLINTON *is a first-year higher education doctoral student at Florida State University in the department of educational leadership.*

INDEX

Aaron, H. J., 88
ACPA (American College Personnel Association), 29–30
ACPA's "Statement of Ethical Principles and Standards," 61–62
Apologizing, 73
Arkin, L. R., 88

Balance, 54–55
Barnes, J., 3, 6
Barr, M., 45, 46
Barr, P., 24–26, 28, 31
Bellah, N. B., 6
Binge drinking, 80
Blimling, G. S., 27, 36, 71, 81, 98
Bridges, W., 84, 85
Brown, H. J., Jr., 59

Campbell, J., 57–58
Cantor, D., 85
Change agent, 46–47
Change/changes: fads and fashion vs. enduring, 38–39; nature of student affairs leadership, 39; personnel, 41–42; reorganization, 40–41; role of student affairs leadership in, 37–38
Chickering, A., 58
Ching, D., 28, 52–53, 66–67
Chopra, D., 57
Community: inner balance role by, 55; as practical wisdom resource, 7–8; relationships within professional, 11–26
Conversations: commitment to other person and, 13–14; developing relationships through, 12–13; generous listening during, 14; giving respect to, 14–15; guiding principles for, 13; having adult, 72; producing value/reputation management during, 15; showing support/speaking truth/focusing on, 14
CSAO (chief student affairs officer): adult transition issues for, 84–85; being fired/making graceful exit, 92; financial planning and, 88–90; forced professional exits and, 87–88; importance of career planning/preparation by, 90–92;

importance of renewal for, 53–54; issues related to retirement/transition from, 83; knowing when to make a transition, 84; reasons for leaving role of, 86–87; retirement and, 88. *See also* Student affairs professionals

Dalton, J. C., 3, 9, 17, 37, 47, 50, 51, 56, 65, 71, 83, 90, 92, 95, 99, 101, 103
Deming, W. E., 77
DeRemer, C., 87, 91
Drinking, 80
DuBois, W.E.B., 69, 70

$E=MC^2$ (energy, media, crisis), 75
Entelechy (guided purpose), 58
Ethics. *See* Professional ethics
External activities, 52–54

Faculty: peculiar people pool making up, 74; taxonomy of college, 75
Fairness value, 70
Financial planning, 88–90
Florida State University, 95
Franklin, A., 25–26
Fraternity membership, 79

Gardner, D. I., 37, 47
Good attitude, 55
Good judgments: associated with profession, 5; of student affairs professional, 3–4

The Handbook of Student Affairs (Sandeen), 25
Head, Heart, and Hands (Pierce College), 57
The Hero with a Thousand Faces (Campbell), 57–58
Higher education institutions: creating memorable student experiences at, 79; investing in learning research by, 79–80; peculiar people attracted to, 74; practical wisdom on operating public, 75–76; strategic planning vs. positioning by, 77–78
Houston, J., 58
Humor, 55

105

Inner balance: attitude and humor for, 55; keeping proper perspective for, 55; role of community in, 55; seeking balance to achieve, 54–55
Inner work, 54–59
Instincts, 20–21
Involuntary Termination: What If It Happens to You? (NASPA), 88

Kozy, M., 88

Learning: investing in research on, 79–80; leading to practical wisdom, 6–7; value of doing for, 74–75
Life planning: financial, 88–90; importance of preparation and, 90–92; importance to student affairs professionals, 83–84; for retirement, 88. *See also* Transition issues
Listening, engaging in generous, 14
Live and Learn, Pass It On (Brown, Jr.,), 59

McClinton, M. M., 101, 103
Mergenhagen, P., 88
Monat, B., 25
Morality/ethics. *See* Professional ethics
MTV, 77

NASPA conference (2001), 21–23
Nuss, E., 15–16, 17, 31, 42, 63, 83, 84, 87, 91, 93

Out of the Crisis (Deming), 77
Outward Bound (Sawtooth Primitive Area), 68–69

Parks, S., 101
Personal development, 49–50
Personnel changes, 41–42
Pierce College, 57
Practical wisdom: community of colleagues resource for, 7–8; competency aspects of, 3; description of, 101–102; drawn from student affairs leaders, 4; learning leading to, 6–7; stories of, 8–9; student affairs success requiring, 101–102; teaching, 7; training vs., 5
Practical wisdom diary: on adult conversations with students, 72; on apologizing as part of the job, 73; on ask what students want, 72; on battles worth fighting, 73; on creating memorable college experiences, 79; on $E=MC^2$, 75; on fading legends, 73; on

fraternity membership, 79; on going along to get along not working, 71–72; on importance of students' interests/needs, 73–74; on influence of national peer norm on student culture, 76–77; on investing in learning research, 79–80; on operating public university, 75–76; on peculiar people attracted to higher education, 74; on renewing credibility with students, 76; on strategic planning, 77–78; on student drinking, 80; on student protests/demonstrations, 78; on taxonomy of college faculty, 75; on value of students' learning by doing, 74–75
Practical wisdom nuggets: attraction of, 95–96; Blimling on blunders and, 98; Roper on moral choices by leadership, 97–98; Sandeen's reflections and, 96–97; simple truths of basic, 96; Thomas on essential traits for student affairs administrator, 99
Profession: good judgments associated with, 5; meanings of, 4–5
Professional communities: developing relationships within, 12–15; as practical wisdom resource, 7–8; quality of relationships within, 11–12; telling our stories within, 15–26
Professional ethics: guiding leaders, 65–70; Roper's practical wisdom nuggets on, 97–98; student affairs leadership challenges for, 61–65
Professional relationships: with boss/supervisors, 17–18, 44–45; constructed within organization, 23–24; developing, 12–15; using instincts in, 20–21; leadership providing structure to, 16–17; quality of, 11–12; stories on building, 15–26
Professional training, 5

Quinn, J. F., 88

Reeves, P. M., 85
Reisser, L., 21–23, 32, 46–47, 49, 59, 61–62
Retirement: financial planning and, 88–90; importance of planning/preparation for, 90–92; making a graceful exit, 92; transition issues of, 88
Roper, L., 11, 26, 32, 44–45, 54–55, 69–70
Roth, D., 58

Sandeen, A., 25, 29, 31, 33–34, 35, 49–50, 51–52, 56–57, 87, 96–97
Sargment, A., 85
Saturday Night Live (TV show), 77
Sawtooth Primitive Area (Idaho), 68–69
Schlossberg, N. K., 85
Schroeder, C., 29, 33, 35, 53–54, 68–69, 83–84, 89, 91, 92, 93
Self-renewal: external activities for, 52–54; importance of, 49–50; inner work for, 54–59; at work, 50–52
Spencer, J., 37
SSAO (senior student affairs officer): balancing personal life and career as, 30; decisions regarding staying/moving to new institution as, 30–35; examining the career path leading to, 27–28; multiple career paths of, 28–30; observations/conclusions regarding, 35–36. *See also* Student affairs professionals
"Statement of Ethical Principles and Standards" (ACPA), 61–62
Stories: of practical wisdom, 8–9; on relationship building, 15–26; told by student affairs professionals, 8–9
Strategic planning, 77–78
Strategic positioning, 78
Student affairs leadership: changes in jobs, 42–44; changes in personnel of, 37–38; changing personnel in, 41–42; fads vs. enduring changes in, 38–39; importance of integrity/morality in, 61–65; matching strengths to institution's needs, 45–46; nature of change in, 39; providing relationship structure, 16–17; relationship between supervisor and, 44–45; reorganization of, 40–41; Roper's practical wisdom nuggets on, 97–98; as successful change agent, 46–47; values/ethics guiding, 65–70
Student affairs professionals: Blimling's practical wisdom nuggets on blunders by, 98; importance of self-renewal for, 49–50; knowledge/good judgment requirements of, 3–4; life planning for, 83–92; practical wisdom required

for successful, 101–102; renewal at work by, 50–52; renewal from external activities, 52–54; response to student protests/demonstrations by, 78; Sandeen's practical wisdom nuggets on, 96–97; as storytellers, 8–9. *See also* SSAO (senior student affairs officer)
Student culture, 76–77
Student protests/demonstrations, 78
Students: adult conversations by, 72; asking what they want, 72; creating memorable college experiences for, 79; drinking by, 80; fraternity membership by, 79; importance of needs/interests of, 73–74; influence of national peer norm on, 76–77; moral/ethical framework for dealing with, 61–70; renewing credibility with, 76; research investing on learning by, 79–80; SSAO commitment to, 35; value of learning by doing for, 74–75
Sullivan, M., 16, 17, 40–41, 64–65

Thomas, W. (Bud), 31, 34–35, 43–44, 61, 70, 99
Thomson, J. A., 7
Toor, R., 95
Transition issues: being fired/making graceful exit, 92; consideration of adult, 84–85; financial planning as, 88–90; forced professional exits and, 87–88; importance of planning/preparation, 90–92; knowing when to make transition, 84; reasons for leaving CSAO role, 86–87; retirement and, 88
Trexler, A., 95, 99

University of Maryland-College Park, 43–44
University of North Carolina-Chapel Hill, 79

What Do You Want to Do When You Grow Up? Starting the Next Chapter of Your Life (Cantor), 85
Who Moved My Cheese? (Spencer), 37

Back Issue/Subscription Order Form

Copy or detach and send to:

Jossey-Bass, A Wiley Company, 989 Market Street, San Francisco CA 94103-1741

Call or fax toll-free: Phone 888-378-2537 6AM–5PM PST; Fax 888-481-2665

Back issues: Please send me the following issues at $27 each
(Important: please include series initials and issue number, such as SS94)

1. SS _____

_____

_____

$ _____ Total for single issues

$ _____ SHIPPING CHARGES: SURFACE

	Domestic	Canadian
First Item	$5.00	$6.50
Each Add'l Item	$3.00	$3.00

For next-day and second-day delivery rates, call the number listed above.

Subscriptions   Please ❑ start ❑ renew my subscription to *New Directions for Student Services* for the year 2____ at the following rate:

	Individual	Institutional
U.S.	❑ Individual $65	❑ Institutional $130
Canada	❑ Individual $65	❑ Institutional $170
All Others	❑ Individual $89	❑ Institutional $204

$ _____ Total single issues and subscriptions (Add appropriate sales tax for your state for single issue orders. No sales tax for U.S. subscriptions. Canadian residents, add GST for subscriptions and single issues.)

Federal Tax ID 135593032   GST 89102 8052

❑ Payment enclosed (U.S. check or money order only)

❑ VISA, MC, AmEx, Discover Card # _____ Exp. date_____

Signature _____ Day phone _____

❑ Bill me (U.S. institutional orders only. Purchase order required)

Purchase order #_____

Name _____

Address _____

_____

Phone_____ E-mail _____

For more information about Jossey-Bass, visit our Web site at: www.josseybass.com

PROMOTION CODE = ND3